Transport Economics
in Developing Countries

Transport Economics in Developing Countries

Pricing and Financing Aspects

A. R. Prest

Stanley Jevons Professor of Political Economy and Cobden Lecturer, University of Manchester

Assisted by Norman Lee Lecturer in Economics, University of Manchester

WEIDENFELD AND NICOLSON
5 Winsley Street London W1

SBN 297 17776 1

Printed in Great Britain
by Ebenezer Baylis and Son Limited
The Trinity Press, Worcester, and London

Contents

List of Tables

Preface

This book stems from work originally done for the Transport
Research Program of The Brookings Institution, Washington,
D.C., on the basis of a grant from the Agency for International
Development. So my first duty is to give full acknowledgment
to this stimulus. Next, I must express deep gratitude to Dr
Norman Lee, of the University of Manchester, who gave a very
great deal of assistance both in the United Kingdom and in
visiting Kenya, Uganda and Ethiopia collecting information.
I also wish to thank a number of people in India and Nigeria –
particularly Dr A. Adedeji in the latter case – who helped me
when in those countries. Finally, there are a number of others
both in the United Kingdom and the United States, too
numerous to name, to whom I am indebted for most valuable
help in a great variety of ways.

A.R.Prest
Manchester, April 1968

A*

1 Introduction

When the history of the economic thought of the twenty years or so after the second world war comes to be written (or programmed, or whatever the relevant technique is at the time), one of the outstanding features for comment will surely be the growing importance, both absolutely and relatively, of the economics of developing countries. In fact, the cynic might say that the growth rate of the literature was far greater than that of the countries themselves. At the same time, despite this escalation of effort there are a number of gaps in the literature; and one of the more obvious is the economics of public enterprises in such countries. There have been innumerable books, symposia and the like on the principles of investment in the public sector – sometimes in its own right, sometimes as part of national plans and so on.[1] There is by now a sizeable volume of literature on the public finances of such countries.[2] The administrative aspects of public corporations have also been aired from time to time.[3] But, despite this welter of advice, good, bad or indifferent, on so many of these closely related topics, there have been fewer attempts to examine the pricing policies of public enterprises of different kinds and to analyse the related issues of taxes, subsidies and loans in respect of such organisations. This seems to be a deficiency. On the one hand, the public sector in such countries

1

(whether in the shape of a government department or a public corporation) is frequently responsible for the provision of services of a commercial character (electricity, water, transport, communications, etc.) and so the direct relevance of public enterprise economics is often greater than in western countries. On the other hand, there is by now a great body of literature in this field concerned with both the theoretical aspects and also with the practical experience of western countries.

In these circumstances, it seemed worth while to investigate some of the issues of transport economics in developing countries. The qualifications in the preceding sentence must be underlined. In this monograph we are not pretending to explore more than one small part of a very large area. We are concerned only with some aspects of transport and only with some countries.

More specifically, we intend to proceed as follows. We shall first sketch in the general background of the principles of charging consumers of public enterprise services. This will cover some of the complications of pricing on the basis of marginal costs, the linkages with investment decisions, the desirability and undesirability of deficits, and so on. Although a good deal of what we have to say is of fairly general application, we shall develop it specifically within the context of transport, and mainly road and rail rather than water or air transport. As we are treading some pretty well-worn paths we shall not attempt to present more than a summary of the important points.

We then move to the reasons why one may wish to temper the application of these general principles. This enables us to cover such issues as externalities, income distribution, regional development and more general growth matters.

Chapter 3 starts on entirely different lines, setting out actual transport pricing practices and the overall financial position of public sector transport in some selected countries. Contrasts are then drawn between the actual position in these countries and the general principles adumbrated in chapter 2. Finally, the plausibility of possible reasons for such differences is examined. Appendices supply further factual information.

In chapter 4 we turn to various policy issues. After setting out the broad objectives and the administrative framework within which operations are likely to be conducted, we discuss direct charges on users, the possibilities of charging non-user beneficiaries from transport services, the various means of subsidy (grant, loan, etc.) from government, the desirability of earmarking special funds for transport purposes, etc. This chapter ends with general conclusions and some appendices on points of detail.

Some of the limitations to our field of inquiry will be obvious from the above but nonetheless we must spell them out more explicitly. We are not dealing *in extenso* with the whole transport sector but only with that part into which government enters financially. This means that we are not directly concerned with the large primitive sector which one often finds (e.g., canoe transport, head loading, bicycle- and animal-drawn transport – except insofar as any of these modes of transport impose costs on or pay duties to the government in one form or another). On the other hand, we are not confined to those cases where transport provision is completely within the public sector (e.g., state railroads or nationalised industries operating over public roads); we are very much interested in those cases where transport is a combination of public and private endeavour (e.g., private buses or trucks operating on publicly provided highways).

Some further points should be made. First, we shall assume throughout most of the discussion that the particular divisions currently found between public and private provision are essentially fixed. We do not attempt to discuss in any detail how the boundaries between public and private provision should be determined. Second, many discussions of transport economics are couched in terms of overall social costs and benefits; for example, Winch[4] classifies road transport costs under the following headings:

1. Fixed highway costs (e.g., construction and maintenance).

2. Vehicle operating costs (e.g., maintenance and running costs, but excluding taxes, such as those on fuel).
3. Users' personal costs (e.g., time taken on journeys).
4. Community costs (e.g., loss of amenity).

For an analysis of all economic aspects of road transport it is obviously necessary to assess costs in some form such as this and to compare the totality of these costs with the demand for road services. Our purpose is different, however. We are primarily concerned with public sector economics – whether receipts of public agencies from private road (or rail, etc.) users cover costs or not, and what can or should be done about the relationships between revenue and costs. We are further involved to the extent that the private transport sector is imperfectly competitive or to the extent that private operators or users impose third party costs or benefits which require government fiscal intervention. But this is the limit of our involvement: we are more interested in the relationship between cost and demand schedules from which privately incurred costs have been netted out than between gross costs and gross demand.

Another way in which our analysis and arguments are limited is that we are not primarily concerned with the details of investment planning. Many absorbing issues arise here but partly for reason of space and partly because they are amply documented elsewhere,[5] we shall not be much concerned with them. The financial background to and consequences of particular investment decisions (e.g., the need for additional government subsidies or for raising loans) are very much our concern, but not the detailed reasons for particular decisions (e.g., the principles on which one should value time savings accruing to users of a new highway).

Another point is that we are explicitly *not* making a series of detailed case studies of particular countries. We shall draw on various countries for specific illustrations of our themes but we do not pretend that we are making an exhaustive study of the transport system or potentialities of any one particular country.

4

Most of our illustrations will be drawn from British Commonwealth countries, but there are reasons for thinking that this is not too much of a restriction. By and large, British Commonwealth countries tend to be in the middle of the spectrum in respect of the ratio of road charges to costs; so they are likely to be a better general source for examples than, say, those in Latin America (with very low charges relatively to costs) or the ex-French territories of Africa (with very high ones).

Notes

1 See, e.g., Paul N. Rosenstein-Rodan, *Capital Formation and Economic Development*, Allen and Unwin, London, 1964; S. Chakravarty, *The Logic of Investment Planning*, North-Holland, Amsterdam, 1959; Jan Tinbergen, *Central Planning*, Yale University Press, New Haven, 1964.

2 See, e. g., Richard Bird and Oliver Oldman, *Readings on Taxation in Developing Countries*, Johns Hopkins Press, Baltimore, 1967; John F.Due, *Taxation and Economic Development in Tropical Africa*, MIT Press, Cambridge, 1963; A.R.Prest, *Public Finance in Underdeveloped Countries*, Weidenfeld and Nicolson, London, 1962; Organization of American States Joint Tax Program, *Fiscal Policy for Economic Growth in Latin America*, Johns Hopkins Press, Baltimore, 1965; Ursula K.Hicks, *Development Finance*, Clarendon Press, Oxford, 1965.

3 See, e.g., A.H.Hanson, *Nationalisation*, Allen and Unwin, London, 1963.

4 David M.Winch, *The Economics of Highway Planning*, Toronto University Press, Toronto, 1963.

5 See, e.g., A.R.Prest and R.Turvey, 'Cost Benefit Analysis: A Survey', *Economic Journal*, December 1965; also references mentioned there.

2   General Principles

The Basic Proposition

As a preliminary to subsequent discussion, it is necessary to set out the general principles of public enterprise pricing. It is usual to start by taking a period of time of such length that no question of replacement of capital equipment arises. It is also convenient to assume initially that one is concerned only with minor adjustments of output, and that such questions as that of closing down altogether rather than continuing in production or that of making major extensions to capacity do not arise.

In these circumstances, the conventional argument on public enterprise pricing runs as follows (all references are to figure 2·1,[1] p. 8). There are a number of ways in which one can relate costs and output, but the first customary distinction is between variable costs and fixed costs (i.e., between those costs whose total varies with changes in output and those whose total does not). The latter are shown by AFC, a rectangular hyperbola; the former by MVC and AVC, MVC showing marginal variable costs and AVC average variable costs. The precise shape of AVC is a matter for some argument, but it is often maintained that it will tend to fall as output increases from a very low level (e.g., through more intensive usage of some indivisible input) and to

7

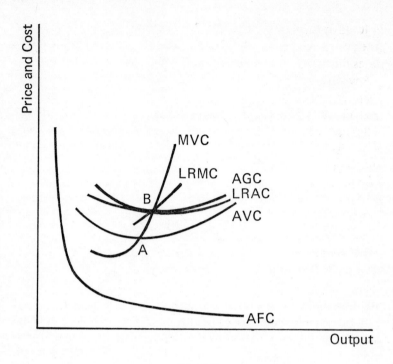

Fig. 2·1

rise again once output expands to a high level (due to, e.g., excessive strain on plant). But, whatever the precise shape of AVC and MVC, we shall find that the latter falls and rises faster than the former. AGC (average global costs) is derived by vertical summation of AVC and AFC. MVC will intersect AVC and AGC at their lowest points.

Leaving aside for the moment LRMC and LRAC, the first proposition is that any public enterprise should equate prices of products to MVC. Only in this case will the marginal value of output to consumers be equal to the alternative use value of the resources engaged. If price is set at a lower level, output will be greater than optimal and too many resources will be engaged in that activity; if price is set at a higher level, the converse will

8

hold. In applying this principle, it is necessary to take account of (the present value) of any costs consequentially incurred at later dates during the planning period.

Several more points should be noted about this proposition. First, it only holds fully for any one industry on the assumption that all other industrialists operate on similar principles, both in selling goods and in hiring factors. Second, it is assumed at this stage that various side effects such as third party effects ('externalities') or consequences of calling on general government revenues to finance deficits can be ignored. Third, strict adherence to the principle can lead to great volatility in prices if demand suddenly changes or if there are major discontinuities in variable costs. Even the strictest devotees of the principle usually temper it by saying that averaging is needed either for administrative reasons or because the time taken by consumers to react may be longer than the intervals between price changes which strict adherence to the rule would dictate.

A further point to note – and this applies to other versions of marginal cost pricing as well as the very simple one we are dealing with at the moment – is the relationship to the benefit principle familiar in the literature of public finance.[2] Confusion is liable to arise in this matter because public utility pricing systems based on the maximum which the traffic will bear are sometimes referred to as 'charging according to benefits'. The distinction here is simply that between total and marginal benefits. Whereas a system of price discrimination approximates in the limit to one of charging according to total benefit (in that total revenue is then equal to the whole area under the demand curve[3] and consumers are deprived of all consumers' surpluses) a system of marginal cost pricing secures the equality of benefits with costs at the margin (in that if price, taken as equal to marginal benefit, exceeds marginal cost there will be an incentive to expand output until any difference is eliminated).

Finally, we have to ask about the shape of the appropriate demand curve. Harrod has argued strongly[4] that most firms do, and on balance should, look at long-run rather than short-run

9

demand curves – the former being more elastic at more points than the latter – even in taking short-run pricing decisions. The same principle will surely apply to public enterprises. They are usually subject to some kind of government regulation on prices and as such procedures are usually lengthy one cannot initiate them all that often. Furthermore, they tend to be conscious of a public image of respectability, conformity to established norms and practices, permanence, and so on. If the relevance of a long-run demand curve is accepted, then the need for observance of the standard pricing rule is all the greater in that, with greater elasticity of demand than in the case of short-run curves, the greater will be the impairment of resource allocation in the case of departures from the rule.

Transport Applications

So much for very general principles. What do they entail in the case of transport? The first and most general point is that they imply that prices should be fixed on the basis of marginal operating costs and that no notice should be taken of fixed costs. So in railroad pricing the relevant question is what incremental costs are incurred by conveying e.g., an extra ton of coal; the interest charges on existing debt are irrelevant. Similarly, with roads, one has to ask what additional maintenance costs result from their usage by an extra truck or bus. At the same time, discontinuities are particularly obvious – the classic example is that of the extra railway passenger who could be responsible for anything from zero additional cost, if he could find an empty seat in a train which was running anyway, to the provision of an extra coach or even an extra train.[5] This ties up with another point. We emphasised that the simple argument about marginal variable costs assumes a given stock of capital. When the capital stock consists of a large number of items rather than a single one, this notion becomes very complex in that if we only allow a very short time to elapse none of the stock will be variable whereas a slightly longer time will allow some to be variable but not the remainder. Even the notion of length of time is not really the fundamental issue; the really crucial point is that of expenditure commitments or contracts which have already been undertaken. The longer the time period one looks ahead the smaller is likely to be the element of commitment and the larger that of variability; but there is clearly no simple relationship between length of time and degree of commitment – it may vary for the same enterprise at different points in time or between different enterprises at the same point in time.

There are many more complications. To illustrate, rather than to treat exhaustively, one must take into account any effects of decisions about pricing of current outputs on both the costs of and demand for future output within the given time horizon. In addition to these issues of temporal linkages, there are also those of system linkages. For instance, it may be sensible to price the usage of a rail or road feeder service below marginal cost if a higher figure would mean a reduction in usage of a main line or main trunk route and hence a smaller incremental return for the system as a whole. Similarly, it is not necessary that prices should cover the marginal costs of transport from A to B and those from B to A separately; insofar as the two journeys can be regarded as a joint product,[6] the only necessary requirement is that the price for the two together should cover the marginal cost of the joint operation.

The problem of cost definition is intensified by the difficulty of defining a standard quality in a service industry like transport. Pinning down the marginal variable costs of providing road space for an additional lorry depends on one's ability to say, *inter alia*, when the standard of a road's surface is kept constant; and the marginal variable costs of carrying an extra passenger on the railway might appear to be constant but would in effect be rising sharply if the discomfort of travel rose sharply due to more passengers being crowded together.

Despite these difficulties of interpretation of the general principle, it has now been argued for a long time that, by and large,

11

transport pricing should be based on it. Wicksell, for instance, said:

The size of the resulting deficit is immaterial in this connection, that is to say, it is irrelevant for the economic justification of the price reduction . . . Any surplus of revenue over cost would be even less acceptable. The existence of such a surplus as, for example, the spectacular profits of the Prussian State Railways, may be a shining testimony to the efficiency of the administration and to the prosperity of the industrial and commercial life of the country; but at the same time the surplus also indicates that the enterprise is far from its optimum degree of utilisation both in national and individual terms. The passenger and freight traffic of the Prussian State Railways would probably increase very considerably with an appropriate reduction in rates. Everyone would gain thereby and no one need lose, provided only that the ensuing deficit be financed by taxes in a suitable manner.[7]

It is easy to see why people have felt in this way. If we predicate a long-run demand curve, the possible wastes of not conforming to the marginal variable cost principle become especially high, as we not only have the more obvious failure to use existing capacity to the best advantage[8] but also the point that decisions about the location of plants and factories may be adversely affected. However, elasticity of demand depends, as always, on the degree of substitutability between products and so the chances of undesirable repercussions are less if one is looking at pricing policy for the whole transport system rather than at a single means of conveyance between two particular points. They are also less if public transport charges are only a small part of total costs.

Finally, one must be clear that the assumption of marginal variable cost being equal to price throughout the rest of the economy is most unlikely to be valid. There is no short cut prescription for amending the formula in such cases, but we shall return to some of the complications later.

The Closing-Down Case

Our analysis so far has been confined to marginal costs on their own but now we must consider them in relation to other cost concepts. First, what are the consequences when marginal variable costs are less than average variable costs, AVC, as in the case of low levels of output in figure 2·1? It is often argued that if the demand situation is such that pricing on a MVC basis would not cover AVC, the firm should cease operations.[9] All due allowance must, of course, be made for the repercussions of such a move – expected costs of restarting if there is any possibility of demand improving, loss of customers if supply is intermittent, etc. Subject to such modifications, the portion of the AVC curve to the left of A, the point of intersection with MVC, can be thought of as being the appropriate marginal curve relevant to decisions about whether to produce or not – in the sense that it shows the savings which can be made by ceasing operations altogether.

Two major comments have to be made on this notion. First, if there are non-marginal changes in the process of shutting down, the fundamental criterion on which the decision to produce, or not to produce, should be taken is not the comparison between changes in total revenue and in total costs, but rather that between changes in total utility and in total costs. This is a well-known point going back (at least) to Marshall's *Principles* and reiterated on a number of occasions.[10] If the position is as shown in figure 2·2 (p. 14) where OFBC shows the total utility from producing OC and OEGC the total cost, then production is preferable to closure (even though the demand curve lies below AVC throughout) provided that AFB exceeds AEGB in size. The essential point in a case of this sort is that *if* it were possible to discriminate perfectly between consumers, total revenue *could* then be greater than total costs.[11] For the moment, we shall leave on one side the practical importance of this sort of case in the transport field and return to it later.

The second major comment is that decisions about closing

13

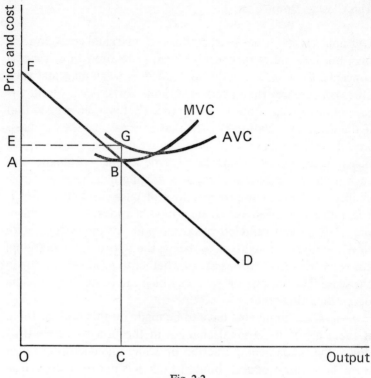

Fig. 2·2

down or opening up production may be related to those about capital investment. In some cases, the decision whether to close down or continue may have no implications for the state or condition of an undertaking's capital equipment; but it is also possible to envisage a situation where capital equipment is more or less worn out and where the decision whether or not to continue production is indissolubly linked with whether or not to replace capital equipment. This is one facet of the old tag that in the long run all costs are prime costs. All we want to do at this stage is to draw attention to this link between variable cost price theory and capital investment decisions – we shall return to it in more detail later.

14

Other Reasons for Deficits

Returning to figure 2·1, we have now dealt with some of the issues arising when MVC < AVC. We now look at other points on the MVC curve and start with B. If the demand curve intersects the cost curve here, it is a point of both short- and long-run equilibrium; short-run in the sense that output at that level satisfies the MVC = Price condition and long-run in the sense that not only is the sum of average fixed (AFC) and average variable (AVC) costs (=average global costs, AGC), covered but so also are long-run average and long-run marginal costs.[12] If the demand curve does in fact pass through B there will in general be a case for renewing capital equipment of the same capacity, neither more nor less, whenever necessary.[13]

If the demand curve, however, cuts MVC at a point to the left of B, we then come to the general problem of public enterprise deficits – in that if output is determined on the MC = Price principle, average revenue must be less than average global costs. There is one point to note before we face up to this issue, however: if the decision-making period is so long that there are no fixed commitments, we then have a state of affairs where all costs are variable. In that case we no longer have a divergence between AVC and AGC (and also LRAC and LRMC become superfluous). We are therefore left with only MVC and AVC (both drawn on a new scale) and no problems of losses arise (unless demand is so small that price lies below AVC). In that case, we are back to the same prescriptions as in the short-term variable cost case.[14] Leaving that possibility on one side, it will be apparent that pricing on the basis of marginal variable cost will lead to a deficit. Before considering the finance of this deficit, let us look at the implications for replacement of the capital stock. Obviously, the normal expectation would be that if losses have been incurred, then at the very least there will be a contraction of the capital stock when the time comes for renewal, or, perhaps, even a complete shutdown, depending on expected future demand. But once we contemplate large changes in output

15

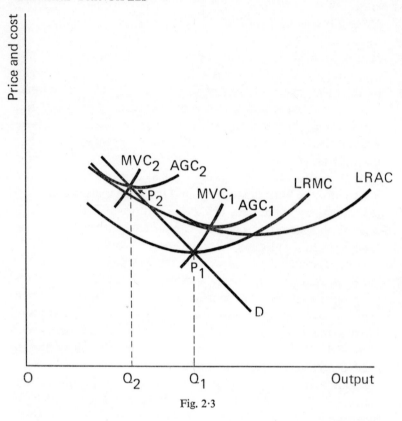

Fig. 2·3

of this sort, we have to resort to the total benefit–total cost principle. In other words, whilst a calculation in terms of average revenue and average cost might give one size of plant when investment decisions are taken, a contemplation of average utility and average cost might give us a larger one. In the latter case, the result will be a persisting deficit which will have to be met by one means or another.

The standard illustration of this kind is when LRMC is downward sloping; this is a highly important and relevant case in many transport situations (e.g., the provision of mass transit). Figure 2·3 above shows the position.

Suppose we start from P_1, the point of intersection between

16

the demand curve on the one hand and MVC_1 and LRMC on the other. Price would be less than AGC_1 and so a deficit would be incurred. One would then expect to see plant size and output contracted, say, to P_2, the point at which D intersects MVC_2. This would now mean that average global costs AGC_2 are covered.[15] But if we view the change as one which must be decided on a utility–cost basis rather than a revenue–cost basis, it is then perfectly possible that the decision to contract cannot be justified.[16] We have therefore a case in which a deficit persists even though it could be avoided. In other words, what started as a position of unavoidable loss ends as one of avoidable loss. The principles on which such a deficit should be met will be explored shortly but in the meantime it should be noted that it is not the presence of scale economies *as such* which makes the deficit persist, but the application of utility rather than revenue considerations.

The Finance of Deficits

It would appear therefore that there are two distinct reasons why a public enterprise operating on a MVC basis may be running at a loss at any one time. First, there may be an unintentional loss – the potential demand over-estimated, capital equipment too big, etc. Second, there may be an intentional one – in the sense that total benefits or utility calculations predicate a larger capital equipment than will allow a surplus, given the usual MVC pricing principle.[17] In practice, it may be extremely difficult to distinguish the two components (e.g., an intentional deficit may unintentionally increase in size) but analytically it is most important to do so.

A deficit of the first type must be due to an unforeseen shift of the demand curve or of the marginal variable cost curve, or both, making some capacity redundant. In these circumstances, the natural thing would be to say that the penalty of the mistake should fall on producers, by analogy with what would happen

17

in a privately owned industry. In that case it may be possible to draw on reserves for a limited period, but sooner or later stock-holders will feel the draught. But as public utilities frequently do not have equity stock, there may be no equity shareholders to take part or all of the strain. Nor does one expect to find such categories as holders of preference stocks, who can be squeezed if a mistake of this sort occurs in private industry. Indeed, it is precisely the fact that public utility stocks are deemed to be free of that sort of risk which allows them to be issued at lower coupon rates than large industrial issues of similar standing and maturity. The upshot is that one is forced back to government subsidies of one sort or another, until such time as the industry has contracted sufficiently to obviate the need for them. How-ever, there are at least three reasons why such a financial solu-tion may be undesirable. First, the subsidy from public funds can only come from more public revenue, more borrowing or less spending; it is all too easy to forget that the consequences of any one of these courses of action for the supply of total resources of their allocation between different ends may be substantially worse than the loss of benefits to consumers through paying a price higher than MVC for the consumption of transport ser-vices. Second, it may be judged that on income distribution grounds there is a stronger case for meeting the deficit out of the pockets of transport consumers rather than from those who would pay the higher taxes or receive less benefits from govern-ment spending. This might be the case if, for instance, the only possible immediate way of raising more government revenue was excise taxes on articles of mass consumption. Third, there are various administrative reasons why one may not wish to go the whole hog. There is the well-known argument that, once started, government subsidies breed expectations of further sub-sidies and so are conducive to inefficiency in management. There is also the danger that organised labour pitches its demands for wage increases that much higher if it thinks that the public purse can be drawn on for this purpose.

For reasons of this kind, one may wish to saddle the particular consumers of a service with some of the losses due to unintentional over-equipment. What about the case of intentional over-equipment? Here the answer would seem to depend on whether the excess of total utility over total cost is derived solely from considering benefits to the current generation of consumers or whether their successors' welfare is also being taken into account. Once again this distinction may be difficult to quantify in practice but at least we must discuss the principle.

If we are only concerned with the present generation of consumers, it would seem reasonable to argue that charges on them should, by one means or another, be high enough to prevent a deficit emerging. If the deficit is due to selecting capacity size on the criterion of total utility exceeding total costs, then by definition it is the consumers of that service who are gaining from this decision and it is hard to see why the burden of deficit finance should be borne by tax-payers at large.[18] There is endless scope for argument about the best way of covering such costs. Discriminatory charges are one method – and allegedly[19] a very traditional one in railway rate making. However, there are both economic and political limits to this method. Even when discrimination is easy between different consumer groups and/or different units of consumption it may be unwise to make it severe; and practices which border on being inquisitorial (and this may be the only means of making discrimination work effectively in some cases) are liable to be resented and to be attacked through political or other channels. Another method is the two-part tariff type of arrangement, whereby each consumer pays a fixed or quasi-fixed sum as well as according to the amount consumed. The major snag about such a device is that 'entry charges' of this sort are likely to keep out some consumers and so reduce consumption below what it would be purely on marginal cost considerations and so, in turn, reduce the usage of capacity to less than the optimum. A straight *per capita* standing charge might also be attacked as being a regressive tax, but this difficulty can sometimes be avoided by relating the standing charge to income. A third device is to say that consumers should

19

be charged on the basis of LRMC and not MVC. This will automatically secure that some account is taken of capital charges as well as variable costs. But deficits are not necessarily eliminated thereby; and this principle is again subject to the attack that it may cut usage of existing resources to an unwarranted extent.

These are the sorts of devices which can be used to make consumers pay for an intentional deficit – or for that matter, an unintentional one, if it is judged that the burden in such a case should lie on consumers rather than taxpayers. All of them are practicable, provided one is willing to make approximations, sometimes pretty large ones. All are capable of application to transport, e.g., a railway might discriminate, or it might construct a fare structure on the basis of a station charge plus a mileage charge, or it may load short-term marginal cost with a capital charges factor. But there are no unique principles for choosing between them in that everyone will have different ideas about the relative merits of a slightly differing income distribution and a slightly differing usage of existing capital equipment. And all of them may be weak instruments when benefits are widespread and diffused rather than concentrated on a small and discernible body of consumers.

Finally, what if a larger capacity than can currently be operated without a deficit is installed in order to cater for the welfare of a future generation as well as the present one?[20] This is a common phenomenon, e.g., a road may be built to a certain specification not just on account of traffic at the moment but with an eye to what it will be a few years hence; or a breakwater may have to be built to cover a whole port area even though the initial number of berths and amount of traffic are insufficient for profitable operation. We shall come to these points in more detail later; at this stage we are only inquiring about the finance of deficits incurred for such reasons. In this case, it does not seem reasonable to argue that the current deficit should be met entirely by the present set of users. There is surely a case for some finance from general government revenue. This is an example of a

20

collective decision which involves the sacrifice of some current consumption in order to build capital equipment which will augment future consumption and so should be financed in the same way as other such decisions. In practice, there are inevitable difficulties of separating one generation from another – some people must always straddle both – but the principle is clear.

There is a further point about the provision of finance from general funds for such purposes; if one accepts any of the arguments that the burden of debt rests on future generations,[21] there would be a case for saying that government funds should be raised by debt issue rather than by taxation in that the burden would then fall on the beneficiaries from the project. We should then have the following set-up: the element of benefit to future generations should be financed by government debt-raising and the element of benefit to the present generation should be financed by user charges (unless there are strong arguments to the contrary in the case of the latter).

Public Enterprise Surpluses

We now come to another possibility about the relationship of the demand curve to the MVC curve on figure 2·1, i.e., where it intersects it at a point above and to the right of B. A surplus is now earned as MVC exceeds not only AVC but also AGC and LRAC.

The problems arising in this case are seen most easily if one takes the limiting case where capacity is rigidly fixed. This is less realistic in the transport world (where it is very difficult to say when the last possible passenger or the last pound of cargo has been squeezed in) than it is in many types of manufacturing industry. Nevertheless, this limiting case does show up the issues in sharp relief. Figure 2·4[22] (p. 22) sets out the essentials.

If the demand curve intersects MVC_1 on its vertical section, price has to be fixed at P_1 if rationing or some similar device is to be avoided. This sort of case could arise continuously if

21

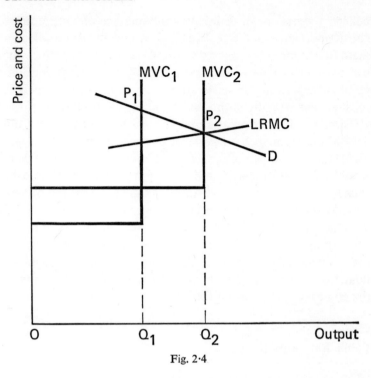

Fig. 2·4

demand were always in excess of any given capacity; or it could arise intermittently if there were marked peaks in consumption as with, say, electricity or transport demands at particular times in particular weeks of the year. To the extent that we ever find ourselves in this situation the short-term pricing rule adumbrated so far needs slight emendation: i.e., instead of saying that price should be fixed at MVC, one must say price should be at MVC or at a higher level if this is necessary to restrain consumption to the maximum output possible.

It can be shown that, in both the case where one has peaks of consumption and in that where one has constant demand, there is complete harmony between pricing on a MVC basis, pricing on a LRMC basis and making investment decisions on the usual criteria of comparing the present value of incremental

22

benefits and of incremental costs. This can be seen in the constant demand curve case, by taking the contrast between P_1 and P_2 on figure 2·4. The short-term pricing rule tells us that if we are operating on MVC_1, price should be fixed at P_1. This will restrict consumption to OQ_1, the maximum output possible with the existing plant. But if price is fixed at P_1, it is in excess of LRMC, the curve showing incremental costs when time is allowed to vary all inputs as need be. The excess of price over LRMC is a signal to expand plant size. Equilibrium is reached at point P_2 where price not only equals MVC_2 (the marginal variable cost experienced with the larger capacity plant) but also LRMC. We can then say that equilibrium price P_2 and output OQ_2 are *either* the result of applying the short-period pricing rule and the normal investment criteria *or*, if one prefers, the result of applying a pricing rule based on LRMC. The three criteria are in the last resort indissolubly linked.[23]

In the case of intermittent demand, the exposition is somewhat more complicated, as one then has to allow for the pricing of off-peak demand at MVC only and the loading of all the capacity costs on to peak consumers, but fundamentally the same conclusions follow as above. Insofar as the peaks of consumption are themselves shifted by differential pricing of this kind, it then becomes necessary to modify charges further to take account of this.

It should be noted that the precise way in which charges are fixed will differ from one public enterprise to another even if each operates in a situation where price exceeds marginal variable cost for some, if not all, consumers. Where one has a system like an electricity grid, the only thing that matters is whether there is peakiness in demand for the system as a whole; insofar as peaks in consumption of single individuals or single geographical areas occur at different times of the day they tend to be unimportant. With transport, it is a different matter. Although peak demands on a given railroad at different times of the day cause no difficulty if they all relate to one kind of transport, the same does not hold in other cases. It is no good having spare passenger rolling stock at night if the main demand is for freight transport. It is no good

B

having a line free from traffic in one geographical area if the main demand is for facilities in another. From this angle of limited substitutability of resources, one would therefore expect fluctuations in transport demands to be greater than in a more closely knit supply system. But clearly this is not the only consideration in an overall assessment. One has to weigh up the relative effects of seasonal variations in consumption, for instance, and these will obviously depend on such matters as climatic conditions (cold winters and/or hot summers providing peaks in electricity demand) or the production structure of the economy (bunching of demands for freight conveyance if agriculture is important and if lifting time coincides for different crops). There are also problems on the production side. Even after allowing for peakiness of hydro-electric output, the likelihood is that seasonal variations in capacity are relatively greater in transport when account is taken of such factors as roads becoming impassable during the rainy season in tropical countries.

Demand Characteristics

How are the characteristics of demand for transport services likely to affect these considerations? Insofar as there are short-term fluctuations in demand for transport services over time, strict application of marginal cost pricing would be likely to imply substantial changes in prices (and, possibly, changes from surplus to deficit) from one year or even one season to another. This in turn might have some undesirable side effects, quite apart from the obvious administrative inconveniences. For instance confidence may be upset in the private sector and so the level of private investment is less than it otherwise would be. And, insofar as investment decisions are taken on the basis of such price movements, these may lead to the application of resources in particular directions (e.g., the location of plants) for a longer period than the shortage or excess of transport capacity might be likely to last.[24] So there are very real issues of settling

24

the optimal degree of smoothing needed in such circumstances.

We now consider longer-term fluctuations in demand. Insofar as one is dealing with countries where real income (even if not real income per head) is growing rapidly it is reasonable to argue that the stock of capital will also be expanding – whether as a cause or an effect is immaterial for the moment. This suggests that over-investment in any given plant size is likely to be a temporary phenomenon only. It may well be the case that there are recurrences of over-investment, whether for intentional or unintentional reasons, as time goes on but at any rate the likelihood of *permanent* over-capacity is reduced.

One must be careful here. The fact that total transport capacity is likely to expand with GNP is no guarantee that transport capacity of any one area will expand at the same rate. There are plenty of countries in the world where railway capacity is standing still or even declining in the face of rapidly growing GNP. There are also plenty of examples of particular regions having too much transport capacity even when this is not so in the rest of an economy. So in no sense should it be thought that all transport investment beyond the immediate needs of the community will have a sort of inbuilt self-righting mechanism. All that can be said is that in a rapidly expanding economy the danger of suffering for long periods from over-investment is much less than in the static kind of case to which our earlier analysis primarily referred. Still less does this argument mean that general government financial problems are lessened. The strain on government finances due to a growing stock of capital can obviously exceed that due to meeting deficits arising from past over-investment. This opens up wider problems to which we shall return.

Inflation

Another subject is the effects of rising price levels. None of us can be certain that the next twenty years will be like the last

25

twenty but nevertheless it seems much more likely that prices in most countries will rise rather than fall. No doubt there will be many technological improvements which could by themselves bring about reductions in prices but one's guess must be that these are likely to be offset by upward movements in money wage rates. So we shall conduct our analysis on that general assumption; it could readily be modified if the reverse proved to be the case. The first effects of rising price levels will be to force both the demand curve and the MVC and AVC curves upwards (figure 2·1). It is tempting then to conclude that this eases the whole 'cost recovery' problem in that AGC, being partly dependent on AFC, will not rise in the same proportion – and indeed, with a given stock of equipment this conclusion will be correct.[25]

When one takes a period long enough to require replacement of capital equipment, the analysis is more complicated. First, one can take the case of an expanding economy with a growing capital stock. Depreciation allowances on the new higher-priced equipment can then be pooled with those accruing from equipment purchased in earlier days and one can easily see that there need not always be crises of finance, when the need arises to replace old equipment, depreciated on its original cost, at a new higher cost.[26]

There is, however, one important kind of case when the problem does not solve itself in this way. Where the stock of capital equipment of, say, a railway system, is constant, or at least where new higher cost capital is not introduced sufficiently quickly to produce a financial counterbalance to the effects of inflation, one can visualise a situation where a price based on MVC would cover AGC but not LRAC – assuming the latter is deemed to take into account replacement and not just original costs of capital equipment. This kind of case received a great deal of attention in the United States, the United Kingdom and other western countries in the first decade after the end of the second world war. By and large, it is not an enduring issue for the private sector of an economy: in that case, failure to charge prices which reflect replacement costs in an industry would be likely to reduce profitability, the industry would become less attractive to investors, output would tend to fall and so prices would rise in the end. But insofar as public utilities do not or cannot operate in this way (e.g., because of obligations to serve 'the public interest') there is an argument for saying that depreciation should be on a replacement cost rather than on an original cost basis. In other words, although the influences on the supply side are likely to be strong enough in the case of the private sector to keep capacity at its appropriate level, in the public sector case one must operate on the demand side via the price system.[27]

Finally, there is an entirely different kind of argument connected with inflation. Insofar as it is thought that cost engendered inflation is an important phenomenon and insofar as the authorities try to operate some kind of prices and incomes policy, there may be an additional reason for subsidising (or at least restraining) prices and charges, whether these relate to intermediate or final services. We shall not discuss the merits and demerits of this approach, but simply list it as an additional possible element in policy.

Price-Marginal Cost Divergences

It is sometimes argued that imperfections of competition in goods and factor markets, especially in developing countries, are so endemic that assumptions about equality of marginal costs and prices are unrealistic and irrelevant. From there the argument often runs that shadow prices based on development plans, which are in turn arrived at by political rather than market processes, should be adopted for many economic calculations. Thus, for instance, it may be argued that one should use lower-than-market prices for labour inputs (reflecting mass unemployment and low marginal productivity of labour) or lower-than-market interest rates (reflecting a lower rate of social than

27

individual time preference) or higher-than-current exchange rates for imports (reflecting over-valuation of the country's currency).

It is a well-known theoretical proposition that when considering pricing policy in one particular industry there is no case for ignoring divergences of marginal costs and prices at other points in the economy and simply proceeding as if they did not exist. At the same time, it is also clear that there is no single, standardised way in which one should proceed.[28] We cannot pretend here to go into the higher rabbinics of these second-best matters, but the following observations seem to be relevant.

Departures from price-marginal cost equalities are likely to depend on such general considerations as the ratio of foreign trade to GNP; the importance of such sectors as agriculture and distribution relatively to others; the role of small independent producers; and the width or narrowness of domestic markets. Too much cannot and should not be read into these criteria (e.g., imports may be subject to physical controls; competition may not be effective among domestic producers even when they do operate on a small scale); they are simply intended as very broad indicators.

Second, the area in which shadow price corrections have to be made may be further reduced the larger the public sector relative to the rest of the economy is. Provided that public sector enterprises price their internal transactions (e.g., sale of government electricity to railways; conveyance of state-mined coal by public road or rail transport) on a marginal cost basis, this will reduce the necessity for reference to shadow prices. The importance of this notion depends on the extent of intra-public sector sales as well as on the relative value added in the public and private sectors. So its practical importance must differ considerably from one country to another.

A third point is that, insofar as corrections to market prices are called for, they may be extremely complex even in principle. It is, for instance, generally accepted by recent writers on cost-benefit analysis[29] that the appropriate technique for approving public sector projects may need to be based on a combination of the social time preference rate (reflecting society's preference at the margin for present goods over future goods) and of the social opportunity cost (reflecting the rates of return, including any capital gains, which would have obtained if the relevant marginal alternative had been investment in the private sector). Neither of these is easy to establish empirically, let alone the appropriate combination.[30]

Another point sometimes made is that when funds are provided from abroad for particular expenditures such as transport, one may have a situation analogous to that of specific capital rationing,[31] where the whole of the allocation has to be spent and so in effect the funds do not have an opportunity cost. However, we suspect that this is a comparatively rare occurrence. There are nearly always economic or political limits to the amount of external funds that a country can obtain over a period of time.

As another example of complexity, take the proposition advanced in the United Kingdom,[32] that UK railways must be subsidised in some of their activities on the grounds that demand for their services has fallen 'unduly' because road users are not charged full social costs. In other words, one should price railway services as if the true cost curve lay below the actual, or alternatively, as if the true demand curve lay above the actual. One can see clearly enough the reasoning behind this second-best proposition (i.e., that the preferable solution of charging road users full social costs is judged to be ruled out), but nevertheless, it would seem to be seriously incomplete as it stands. If railways are subsidised on these grounds, then public revenue must be higher and/or other public expenditure must be lower than would otherwise have been the case. So there must in principle be a whole series of allocative and distributional effects which are concealed behind this seemingly plausible proposition. Unless one is willing to specify precisely what are the fiscal complements to making these subsidy payments, one is only telling part of the story.

Lastly, one must remember that there are administrative costs

29

of taking account of shadow prices. It may require a large central body of overseers to see that each public agency conforms to common principles in allowing for divergences between 'actual' and 'true' costs or prices. But if one does not have much of an overseeing body and leaves it to public authorities to make the adjustments they feel necessary, the results might easily be worse than if there were no adjustments at all.[33]

So by and large we express some caution about the desirability and wisdom of adjusting the prices and/or costs of public enterprises on to shadow bases.[34] Insofar as the practice is justified it may well be that the main adjustment would be to operate on a higher than actual price for capital. Although this would both tend to alter factor input ratios and reduce output below what it would otherwise be, the likely net effect would be an increase in the surplus on operating account.

Externalities

Benefits received by or costs imposed on third parties as a result of public transport provision and use are of many kinds. Standard examples are the change in value of agricultural land made possible by better communications, the potential contribution roads make to defence purposes, the noise and fumes from traffic. But it should be clear from the beginning that not all such third party effects call for modifications to public enterprise pricing policy. First, some benefits may in fact simply be transfers: insofar as a reduction in costs of transport operations on a particular route is passed on to landowners via changes in land rents, there is no necessity for further action by the road authority if it is already charging the direct beneficiaries appropriately. Second, insofar as externalities can be 'internalised' so that the debit and credit entries no longer come in different sets of books, the matter is also settled. Thus, the non-commercial benefits arising from the potential military usefulness of public highways can be taken account of by suitable charging and book-keeping

30

arrangements by the relevant government departments. Finally, if one transport user imposes diseconomies on another, but terms of compensation can be voluntarily negotiated between them,[35] it is unnecessary to have any intervention at government level whether of a regulatory or fiscal character. And even if this is not so, the administrative costs of government intervention may exceed the benefits which may come from it.

So it is by no means the case that all externalities lead to resource misallocation. Nevertheless, there are clearly a number in the transport field which may do. One important case is the effects of transport costs on outputs and prices of intermediate goods, but as this is very complex and has been considered extensively by Tinbergen, Bos and Koyck, and Friedlaender,[36] we shall not discuss it here. Another of the most important in many countries is that of traffic congestion and interaction. The literature on this subject has mushroomed in the last few years[37] almost as fast as the facts of the case and there is no need to go into it fully here.[38] Essentially, one is dealing here with a case where each and every vehicle imposes costs on each and every other vehicle in the form of congestion and delay. One can therefore argue that in principle there is a case for a tax system which makes individuals aware of the costs they are imposing on others, so that uneconomic congestion is eliminated. Alternatively, we can say that failure to charge in this way implies that rent is not being exacted to the fullest extent possible, given the intensive usage of a fixed factor (road space). What precisely should be done with the tax proceeds is more open to argument. They could be used to compensate those who suffer from being forced off the roads; or to relieve road users of other charges; or to make general reductions in taxation or increases in expenditure. The choice between these alternatives will depend on detailed consideration of the distributional and allocational consequences.[39]

We have outlined the congestion issue because of its importance and because it does seem more tractable than some other external relationships. However, there are clearly many others which arise in the transport field, such as noise, smoke, fumes and accidents. Insofar as it is both necessary and practicable to compensate for such relationships by taxes and/or subsidies, one must graft these on to the standard public enterprise pricing principles.

Economic Growth

It is very tempting to argue, both on historical and analytical grounds, that public transport pricing should be subsidised in the interests of economic growth. We find, for instance, statements of the following kind:

... a cheap and extensive system of communications is the greatest blessing which any country can have from the economic point of view.[40]

Economic historians have often argued that transport played a most important role in the nineteenth-century development of Europe and North America.[41] But one should not be swept off one's feet by these arguments. The precise nature of the relationships and the mutual interactions between the variables involved are very difficult to specify, let alone quantify. It is also worth noting that some questions have recently been raised by economic historians themselves about the magnitude of the blessings flowing from the railway developments of the nineteenth century.[42]

Quite apart from the difficulties of analysing what happened historically, one must obviously be cautious about the applicability of such experiences to the present or future problems of societies and countries which are so vastly different. We do not argue that history does not repeat itself and that some of the spectacular nineteenth-century changes in western Europe may not recur; but simply that the same history is unlikely to be repeated in all places and at all times.[43]

32

Let us now look at these matters from a more analytical viewpoint.

Subsidies on public transportation facilities can be deemed to have both general and specific economic effects. Insofar as the subsidy is a net addition to the budget deficit it will have the usual output reactions, primary and secondary, of excesses of government outgoings over incomings. But provisos must be noted. The 'usual reactions' will take the form of extra national output only if there is a supply of unused domestic resources and these will normally need to include skills and capital equipment, as well as unskilled labour. Part of the extra incomes generated may leak abroad in the form of higher imports, visible or invisible. And, insofar as the subsidy on transport is an alternative to subsidies on some other form of government spending or to a general tax cut, rather than a net addition to the budget deficit, these general effects will tend to vanish altogether.

If an economy is already or potentially (e.g., with a larger development programme ahead) in a state of excess demand with rising prices and diminishing foreign exchange reserves, the prime requirement will be a smaller rather than a larger government deficit. The history of many countries in recent years suggests that this is much the most likely state of affairs; and, if so, the call must be for public enterprise surpluses rather than deficits, in the hope that this will lead to a larger total of national saving, after allowing for any reductions in personal and corporate saving as a result of higher fares, freight rates, etc.

The specific effects of cheap public transport facilities are of several kinds.[44] First, there will be a tendency to substitute public transport facilities for private ones, where possible. This might mean, for instance, that publicly owned railroads would attract business from privately owned river steamers; or that the relative importance of small-scale transport activities such as head-loading, bicycles, rick-shaws, bullock carts, canoes, etc., would tend to fall. Second, the pattern of consumption would be affected: there would be substitution of transport-intensive consumption goods (holidays, pleasure travel, etc.) for other

33

goods and services. Third, the pattern of production would be affected in that goods and factors of production are now rendered more mobile. How precisely this would affect the location of industry is, even in principle, very complex: on the one hand, the lower cost of moving goods may make the development of remote areas more feasible, but on the other hand, the greater mobility of labour may attract more people from remote areas to established centres. There are also problems of changes in the relative importance of towns and rural areas in the same district as well as changes between districts. One can be more definite about the ratio of stocks to final output: this can clearly be reduced (with consequential savings in storage space and insurance, as well as capital charges) the easier and faster it is to send goods from one part of a country to another.

Effects of this sort are in principle – and have been in practice[45] – of great importance in stimulating growth rates. But for our purposes we need to know how far they justify subsidies over and above those we have already discussed. We have said that one can justify capital facilities so large that a public utility operates at a loss, provided that the loss of benefits from operating with smaller capital facilities would be greater than the saving in costs.[46] We have also seen that in principle shadow price and externality adjustments can also justify further losses. Once full cognisance has been taken of all these cases, it is not clear that there is anything additional. For the calculation of the benefits on which larger capacity in, say, roads can be justified is essentially a matter of estimating the value of such things as savings of time of men,[47] and of vehicles and their freight contents, including both current and potential usage. If these estimates are made in a comprehensive fashion,[48] they will reflect all the various effects of cheaper public transportation facilities on the pattern of consumption and of production. Similarly, the costs side of the equation reflects the opportunities foregone by diverting more resources into the public transport sector. Once considerations of this sort are married to corrections of market prices on account of externalities and the like, the subject has

34

been covered and it would be duplication (as well as duplicity) to pretend there is anything more to it.

The same general principles hold if we are considering development of a particular region rather than a whole country. Once allowance has been made for the benefit calculations associated with non-marginal changes in output, shadow prices and externalities, there is no *additional* reason for subsidisation – though of course the calculations of benefits and the particular values given to the shadow prices, etc., are likely to differ from those applicable in the whole country case.

Finance of General Government Expenditure

There are a number of types of government expenditure in any country which cannot readily be financed by the specific users or beneficiaries. Quite apart from the much discussed collective goods case, there are other elements such as interest payments on the national debt. There is no unique prescription for saying how much of this burden should be placed on the consumers of the services provided by public enterprises, but insofar as any revenue is raised by indirect taxes to meet these expenditures, there is no reason for exempting public enterprise services from them. There is no simple formula for fixing the size of indirect, rather than direct, taxes for such purposes, but given any specific total for the former, the most reasonable apportionment would seem to be a proportionate distribution among each segment of the economy – making separate calculations in respect of consumers' expenditure, public authorities' current expenditure on goods and services, gross domestic capital formation and exports. To the extent that public enterprises have outputs entering into these categories, they should be taxed accordingly. For this purpose, the proportionate contributions should be the same in respect of each type of service provided by a public enterprise.

Income Distribution

Income redistribution is one of the considerations traditionally influencing the pattern of government revenue and expenditure. Discussion can be endless about how efficiency and redistributional objectives should be combined – e.g., maximise the objective function of efficiency subject to redistributional constraints *or* maximise the objective function of redistribution with efficiency constraints *or* some intermediate policy[49] – but most people would accept that budget decisions should incorporate both elements.

Many issues arise in income distribution. One is that we may simply be dealing with the distribution of income between the class of people who use public transport facilities and the rest of the community. Alternatively, we may be concerned with a particular group of the class of public transport users, differentiated by income, region and so on. A particular example might be that an area has developed in the past because of cheap transport facilities. Any attempt to remove the subsidy element in such cases would then encounter opposition on the grounds that this would subject people to adventitious falls in capital value of property, etc.[50] As another possibility, one might have some combination of group and sub-group policy, e.g., subsidies to one particular sub-group of public transport users, but higher charges to other sub-groups so that the totality of public transport users does not benefit. One should also note that the borderline between the use of public enterprise pricing and the use of taxes as means of income redistribution is a very thin one. One might, for instance, try to increase the surplus on road operations by levying various sorts of user charges – tolls, gasoline taxes, and so on. Alternatively, one can levy very heavy customs and excise duties on private cars, making them progressive with size or value if need be. Formally, one can say that the latter type of taxation is not directly connected with the operation and maintenance of the road system in that the amount of tax paid is independent of road usage, but this is a pretty thin argument –

36

a bit like saying that the amount of tax should be dependent on the number of cigarettes smoked rather than the number bought. Finally, one should remember that income distribution objectives can be pursued by variations in factor input policy (e.g., labour intensive rather than capital intensive methods of production) as well as by product pricing policy.

One must be modest in one's aims in these matters. The traps in tracing out the effects of taxes and/or subsidies on income distribution are often both concealed and deep. These attributes are likely to be particularly marked in the transport sector where many transactions are in respect of intermediate rather than final products. For example, one may have some confidence that a reduction in railway passenger charges benefits certain groups of consumers, but very much less confidence about the distributional effects of changes in freight charges for, say, iron ore, pig iron or steel bars.

A Summing Up

We have tried to set out the elements of public enterprise pricing principles and then bring in some of the complications of second best, externalities, contribution to economic growth, income redistribution, and so on. It is completely impossible to come to any simple conclusion about whether public transport authorities should be operating at a surplus or deficit on current account. Although there are some cases (e.g., capital investment for the benefit of future generations as well as the present one) where a deficit can be defended, there are others (notably the congestion tax case) where one would expect a surplus. Even where current account surpluses are being earned this does not mean that there are no financial problems left. In countries where capital markets are very limited, it would be simply wrong to assume that very much of the finance of net capital investment can be met from the market. Thus, even though sufficient in the way of surpluses is earned to cover replacement of existing capital

37

equipment – and this, as we saw,[51] may require particular attention in periods of rising prices – it may still be necessary to find means of financing net additions to the capital stock. In an economy where the public transport system is developing rapidly, where domestic capital markets are limited, and where there is no easy recourse to foreign sources of finance, whether by way of loan or aid, this state of affairs is only too likely to arise. And when public expenditure already presses extremely hard on revenue, no one can view large financial demands of public enterprise with any equanimity.

It will be noted that, in contrast to some statements on the subject,[52] we have not so far said anything about the need to co-ordinate or integrate public transport facilities. The omission has been quite deliberate: for these terms are so vague that unless they are defined more clearly they are quite meaningless. When further definition is sought, it often transpires that such terms imply the intention of securing the same sort of solution as would come about from the thorough-going operation of a marginal cost pricing system, after making allowances for externalities and the like. If the aims are the same in both cases, any advantages of co-ordination, etc., must lie in the superiority of administrative devices such as licencing, regulations and the like over a competitive pricing system as a method of implementation, e.g., they may be judged to be more thoroughgoing or quicker to operate. These advantages may be substantial in particular circumstances,[53] but there are also likely to be many cases where the advantage lies the other way.[54] Nor should one be deceived by all apparent failures in the pricing system. For instance, one might think of non-duplication of transport facilities along the same route as a sensible aim: and then point to the fact that there are plenty of historical examples of privately built railway lines competing between pairs of cities. But in many such cases the survival of duplicate facilities has been due to a failure to let the consequences of the competitive system work themselves out rather than to the system itself. In other words, the case for administrative devices may rest on the need to correct for the follies and failures of previous administrative devices rather than for basic inadequacies in the competitive pricing system.

However, there are spheres in which this system clearly does not apply, especially those of inter-governmental and intra-governmental relationships. One might, for instance, have a completely 'uncoordinated' road network if each individual local authority were left with complete freedom to route its highways as it wanted. A true interpretation of community preferences for a road system requires deliberations at national level even though the local authorities can share in construction and, if big enough, be wholly responsible for it. And it goes without saying – or should do – that there can also be nonsensical results if the different departments of a single government do not act in unison.

Appendix 2A

Externalities and Congestion Costs

To simplify the argument initially, let us ignore some of the bedevilling complications; we shall take the case of two vehicle firms only[55] and ignore both the reciprocal nature of the externalities and the relationships between the vehicle user class and others. In other words, we will start by looking at the effects of imposing a tax on one vehicle firm, assuming it to be responsible for externalities imposed on the other vehicle-owning firm (but without reciprocity) but on no one else. This is obviously a very artificial construction, but we shall proceed to some more complex cases later. Figure 2·A1[56] shows the position in which A imposes costs on B as it extends output (vehicle flow). If A is oblivious of B's sufferings, it will increase output until its marginal gain (i.e., marginal benefit *less* private marginal cost) is zero (i.e., output would be OF). But if it were possible for A and B to negotiate with one another, the optimal output would be OE, for this is the point at which CD, the net gain curve derived by subtracting B's losses from A's gains, cuts the horizontal axis; any expansion beyond or contraction below this point would mean a smaller net gain. This is therefore the ideal solution which the tax mechanism has to try to emulate. If the tax could succeed in reducing A's output to OE, it would give the same solution as that derived from a compensation process. But we must note what this involves. First, as Turvey has pointed out,[57] it would not be satisfactory if the tax reduced A's output to OE and it was still possible for A and B to bargain. For in this case (assuming the tax proceeds not paid to B) there would be scope for negotiation to reduce output below OE. So in this sort of case the tax will push contraction too far. Whatever the rate at which it is levied, it is bound to lead to a less than optimal output.[58] However, there are other circumstances in which a tax will give the right answer. Schematically, we can say in the case of a tax designed to reduce A's output from OF to OE:

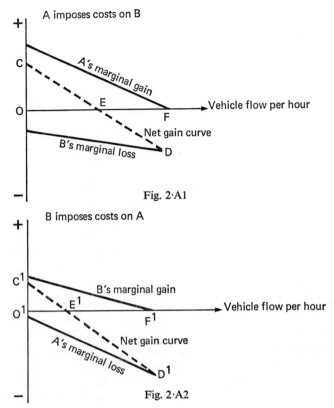

Fig. 2·A1

Fig. 2·A2

Tax proceeds paid to B

A and B free to negotiate: Tax secures optimal. But as this is a substitute for private arrangements (either payment from B to A, or if A is liable, from A to B), the case for it must depend on income distribution, fairness, etc.

A and B not free to negotiate: Optimal unlikely (only secured if B continues to take defensive measures against A's activity, despite receiving tax proceeds).

Tax proceeds not paid to B

A and B free to negotiate: Output reduced below optimal.

A and B not free to negotiate: Optimal can be secured.

41

It should be noted from the previous example that the distribution of the tax proceeds is not crucial to the allocation argument in the sense that an optimal output of A's vehicle flow can be secured whether the tax proceeds are paid to B or not – though there are implications about the non-distorting effects of alternative forms of revenue.

We must now face a difficulty which we have evaded so far – what determines the shape and position of B's marginal loss curve? Coase argues that this partly depends on whether compensation is, or is not, payable. He also makes the point strongly that the relevant computation is not the damage directly due to A's activities, but rather what it costs A in prevention or B in remedial measures. In the smoky chimney context, if a drying machine costs less than the effort of re-washing clothes blackened by smoke, a better measure of loss imposed is the cost of the dryer. In the congestion case, if one man decides to give up travelling rather than be forced down to a low speed by another, the relevant measure is the loss incurred thereby (e.g., the reduction in profits through not making the journey at all or the net costs of making it by some other means) and not the costs of going at the speed at which he would have travelled if he had continued to use his vehicle. This seems right in principle but fiendishly difficult to quantify in practice. It might be noted that empirical work on the congestion tax is usually based on calculations about reduction in speed of traffic flow due to the marginal user and therefore to some unknown extent must misstate the loss involved.

So much for the 'easy' but artificial non-reciprocal case. Now let us ask about the complications when A imposes costs on B, and B on A; we keep up the pretence for the time being that neither A nor B imposes costs on any pedestrians or cyclists. Figure 2·A2 showing the costs imposed by B on A is the non-identical twin to figure 2·A1. If reciprocity were ignored, the reasoning about this figure – natural output O^1F^1, optimum output O^1E^1 – would be exactly the same as in figure 2·A1. So this is straightforward.

What conclusions can be drawn from a simultaneous perusal of figures 2·A1 and 2·A2? We can specify the optimal scale of A's output and the optimal scale of B's output as being OE and O^1E^1 respectively, the total of net gains being greatest for this combination of outputs. But having said that, it is easy to see that the situation is now much more complex. The rate of tax which would cut A's output to OE is not necessarily the same as that which would cut B's output to O^1E^1, but it is obviously impossible to levy differential tax rates in anything more than the simplest kind of case. One negative point comes out of the diagrams: the crude fallacy that, because each vehicle imposes costs on each other vehicle, the situation will right itself without any intervention or negotiation. If one adds together the marginal gain and marginal loss curves either for A or for B, it can be seen that there is no reason why the resultant output in either case should be optimal.

So far we have neglected reactions between motorists and other members of the community. But there are clearly reciprocal relationships among motorists, pedestrians, and cyclists: each category in pursuing its own interests affects those of others. When we also remember the painfully obvious simplification in our analysis of the road-using community – the stock of vehicles being divided between two firms only – we see the complexities of any full analysis allowing for many more vehicle owners and ruling out any possibilities of negotiation.

In these circumstances, it is tempting to give up the game and say quite simply that there are so many complications in the analysis that one should not even try to impose a special congestion tax on vehicles which are, say, entering city central areas. But this does seem to be a counsel of despair; we are clearly likely to get an improvement in welfare after levying a congestion tax even if optimal results are unobtainable.[59]

Notes

1 Based on D.H.Robertson, *Lectures on Economic Principles*, Staples, London, 1957, vol. 1, chapter 12. Clear expositions of the basic principles can be found in many other books on price theory (e.g., Milton Friedman, *Price Theory*, Cass, London, 1962, and Abba P. Lerner, *The Economics of Control*, Macmillan, New York, 1964.)

2 See, e.g., Alan T.Peacock and Richard A.Musgrave, *Classics in the Theory of Public Finance*, Macmillan, London, 1958; Richard A. Musgrave, *The Theory of Public Finance*, McGraw Hill, New York, 1959; James M.Buchanan, *The Public Finances* (2nd ed.), Irwin, Homewood, Illinois, 1965.

3 Diagramatically, total benefit is given by the area OFBC and consumers' surplus by the area AFB in figure 2·2 (p. 14).

4 R.F.(Sir Roy) Harrod, *Economic Essays*, Macmillan, London, 1952, pp. 150 ff.

5 Cf. the well-known discussion by Dessus of the example of the passenger travelling from Paris-Nord to Calais; G.Dessus, 'Rate Fixing in Public Utilities', in James R.Nelson (ed.), *Marginal Cost Pricing in Practice*, Prentice-Hall, Englewood Cliffs, New Jersey, 1964.

6 For a classic discussion of this see A.C.Pigou, *Economics of Welfare* (4th ed.), Macmillan, London, 1932, chapter 18.

7 Knut Wicksell, 'A New Principle of Just Taxation', in Richard A. Musgrave and Alan T. Peacock (eds), *Classics in the Theory of Public Finance*, Macmillan, London, 1958, p. 103.

8 The standard example is Dupuit's bridge. J.Dupuit argued as long ago as 1844 that it was irrational to charge people anything for crossing a bridge when no incremental costs are involved in doing so. Cf. J.Dupuit, 'On the Measurement of Utility of Public Works', *International Economic Papers*, vol. 2 (translated from the French), Macmillan, London, 1952.

9 To reduce total variable costs to zero, it may be necessary to do more than simply cut output to zero (e.g., full savings on

supervisory staff or licence fees might not be realised without further action).

10 Cf. the celebrated paper by Harold Hotelling, 'The General Welfare in relation to problems of Taxation and of Railway and Utility Rates', *Econometrica*, 1938. A particularly clear exposition is to be found in Leif Johansen, *Public Economics*, North-Holland, Amsterdam, 1965, pp. 171ff.

11 Further complications arise in the appropriate definition of costs (see Lerner, *op. cit.*, chapter 16) and also the assumption that one can ever measure total utility but we shall not go into them here.

12 The differences between long-run average costs (LRAC) and average global costs arise from the presumed greater malleability of factors in the long run, making for greater elasticity of supply. The same point applies to the relative slopes of MVC and LRMC (long-run marginal cost) – the more time there is to change relative inputs of different factors the more likely it is that the marginal cost of meeting an increment of output will be less.

13 We return shortly to various complications which arise when LRMC is not equal to MVC at the point where MVC=AGC; and when, e.g., changes in demand and the general price level are taken into account.

14 I.e., if producing, fix price=MVC; and if deciding whether to produce or close down, compare changes in total cost with changes in total utility or in total revenue depending on whether there are indivisibilities in closure or not.

15 Assuming that financial obligations had fallen *pari passu* with the contraction of plant size, e.g., by an appropriate financial reconstruction.

16 Depending on whether the reduction in area under the demand curve is greater than the net reduction in total costs. See G.M. Neutze, 'Investment Criteria and Road Pricing', *The Manchester School*, January 1966.

17 A particular case is where a larger capital equipment than is needed immediately is installed in order to cope with larger demands in future periods. Current losses are then deliberately incurred in the expectation that they will be more than offset by future profits – a very important category of transport investment in many countries.

It should be emphasised that calculations of benefits and costs

45

in situations where all the optimal conditions are not fulfilled (because of, e.g., capital rationing) may become extremely complicated. See Prest and Turvey, *op. cit.*

18 The population of taxpayers will differ from that of transport consumers, not only because some residents will be in one group but not the other; but also because foreigners are much more likely to be in the latter than in the former group.

19 'Allegedly' because data are so scarce in many countries that it is difficult to be certain that charges which apparently discriminate between consumers (in the sense that price/marginal cost ratios differ) do so in fact. We shall return to this point in chapter 3.

20 If total benefits exceed total costs for the future generation, but not for the current one, and if future benefits are independent of current ones, there would be no case for undertaking the project now.

21 Cf. James M. Buchanan, *Public Principles of Public Debt*, Irwin, Homewood, Illinois, 1958, for the first major contribution in recent years; and James M.Ferguson, *Public Finance and Future Generations*, University of North Carolina Press, Chapel Hill, 1964, for a survey of the issues. We shall return to this subject in chapter 4.

22 Based on Marcel Boiteux, 'Peak-Load Pricing', in Nelson, *op. cit.* The issues are further analysed by R. Turvey, 'Marginal Cost Pricing in Practice', *Economica*, November 1964. We are also indebted to Mr Turvey for showing us an unpublished paper in which his ideas are further developed.

23 Cf. Boiteux, *op. cit.*, p. 71. 'Provided there is an optimum investment policy, short-term pricing is also long-term pricing, and there is no longer any contradiction between the two.'

24 Cf. Boiteux, *op. cit.*, p. 71.

25 Assuming that demand curves in general shift upwards with variable cost curves.

26 Cf. Evsey D.Domar, *Essays in the Theory of Economic Growth*, Clarendon Press, Oxford, 1957. Crises may still arise in particular cases of course, e.g., due to depreciation funds being short-earned in earlier years or difficulties in borrowing to finance capacity extensions.

27 The same general point holds in respect of land costs and other non-renewable assets (i.e., the appropriate figure for costing

purposes is current value in alternative uses rather than original purchase price). But where alternative use values are zero (e.g., in respect of the costs of enabling legislation which may have been incurred when, say, a railway started) no account should be taken of such assets. Cf. G.J.Ponsonby, 'Earnings on Railway Capital', *Economic Journal*, December 1960, and A.R.Prest, 'Some Aspects of Road Finance in the UK', *The Manchester School*, September 1963.

28 Cf. E.Mishan, 'A Survey of Welfare Economics, 1939–59', *Economic Journal*, June 1960, pp. 245–6. See also, Ann F.Friedlaender, *The Interstate Highway System*, North-Holland, Amsterdam, 1966, pp. 124–5, for an example of how it is impossible to find an optimum pricing policy for highways when one takes three sectors – highways, railways and other – each with differing price/marginal cost ratios.

29 For a summary see Prest and Turvey, *op. cit.*

30 It might be noted that there is a weakness in the argument advanced by Stephen A.Marglin ('Economic Factors Affecting System Design', chapter 4 of Arthur Maass (ed.), *Design of Water Resource Systems*, Harvard University Press, Cambridge, 1962, pp. 195–6) in furtherance of the interdependence proposition about investment (i.e., that people's time preferences will permit more investment for future generations when it is organised publicly than when it is provided by the market). The argument is as follows. Assume an investment of $1·00 now will make available $2·00 at some given date for a future individual. If the individual operating through the market place today feels that the provision of $1·00 of consumption for the future individual only gives satisfaction equivalent to $0·10 of consumption now there is no inducement to invest. If, however, there is a publicly organised investment programme and each individual is assumed to value $1·00 of a contemporary's consumption as equal to $0·15 of his own, then it is argued that marginal time preference will be given by the formula

$$\frac{1·00+(n-1)\,0·15}{n\,(0·1)}.$$

Provided $n > 17$, this value will be less than 2 and so investment can be justified on time preference principles.

The weakness in this argument is the proposition that the individual continues to value $1·00 of future consumption as equal to $0·10 of current consumption even when virtually all the latter relates to people other than himself. If 0·1 were replaced by a much lower figure the value of the formula would be correspondingly higher and the certainty of the conclusions reduced.

31 Jack Hirshleifer, James C. DeHaven and Jerome W. Milliman, *Water Supply*, University of Chicago Press, Chicago, 1960, pp. 169ff.

32 Ministry of Transport, *Transport Policy*, Cmnd. 3057, HMSO, July 1966, especially paragraph 18. The ideas are given more precise form in Ministry of Transport, *Railway Policy*, Cmnd. 3439, HMSO, November 1967.

33 Cf. Prest and Turvey, *op. cit.*, p. 705.

34 Cf. Sir Arthur Lewis, 'A Review of Economic Development', *American Economic Review*, May 1965, p. 15. 'The only way to achieve decision-making on the basis of a low shadow wage is to have a low actual wage.'

35 It should be noted that misallocation of resources can be avoided *either* by payment from the perpetrator to the sufferer *or* vice versa; the direction of payment is a distributional issue. (See Ronald Coase, 'The Problem of Social Cost', *Journal of Law and Economics*, October 1960.)

36 Cf. Jan Tinbergen, 'The Appraisal of Road Construction: Two Calculation Schemes', *Review of Economics and Statistics*, August 1957; H.C.Bos and L.M.Koyck, 'The Appraisal of Road Construction Projects', *Review of Economics and Statistics*, February 1961; also, Friedlaender, *op. cit.*, chapter 2. Friedlaender's conclusion (p. 15) is that although it cannot be stated positively that vehicular benefits will underestimate social benefits, there is a strong chance that this will be the case if the supply of factors is fairly elastic and commodity substitution is not too great.

37 See Herbert D.Mohring and Mitchell Harwitz, *Highway Benefits*, Northwestern University Press, Evanston, 1962, chapter 2; A.A. Walters, 'The Theory and Measurement of Private and Social Costs of Highway Congestion', *Econometrica*, October 1961; *Road Pricing: The Economic and Technical Possibilities*, Ministry of Transport, London, 1964; G.J.Roth, *A Self-Financing Road*

System, Institute of Economic Affairs, London, 1966; *Road Track Costs,* Ministry of Transport, London, 1968.

38 One way of looking at the problems is outlined in appendix A to this chapter.

39 Cf. J. H. Moore, 'Congestion and Welfare – A Comment', *Economic Journal,* March 1968. Note that there is no reason why the level of road investment should be different in the various cases (assuming the investment calculations take full account of benefits to potential users as well as to current ones) except insofar as the distribution of income changes and this leads to a different level of demand for road services.

40 Federation of Nigeria, *The Economic Programme of the Government of Nigeria, 1955–60,* Sessional Paper No. 2, Lagos, 1956, p. 43.

41 Cf. H.J.Habakkuk and M.M.Postan (eds), *Cambridge Economic History of Europe,* Cambridge University Press, London, 1965, vol. 2, part 1, especially chapter 4, 'Transport', by L.Girard; F.L.Nusbaum, 'History of Economic Institutions of Modern Europe' (an introduction to *Der Moderne Kapitalismus,* by W.Sombart, Crofts, New York, 1935).

42 For two recent examples see Robert W. Fogel, 'Railroads as an Analogy to the Space Effort: Some Economic Aspects', *Economic Journal,* March 1966; and W. Ashworth, 'The Late Victorian Economy', *Economica,* February 1966.

43 To take a single example – with all the risks implied thereby – we find that major road improvements in Ethiopia in recent years have led to substantial reductions in journey times and freight costs and substantial increases in traffic (cf. *Ethiopian Highways,* January 1966). But there is no evidence that this has led to more rapid growth of the economy.

44 Cf. Mohring and Harwitz, *op. cit.,* chapter 1, for extended discussion.

45 Cf. A.J.Youngson, *Overhead Capital,* Edinburgh University Press, Edinburgh, 1967, chapters 4 and 5.

46 Cf. p. 17, above.

47 In principle, one would expect these to be less important in countries with low marginal productivity of labour and hence lower valuation of units of time than in western countries.

48 This may be a complex operation; cf. Bos and Koyck, *op. cit.*

49

49 Cf. Marglin, *op. cit.*, p. 83. These arguments are taken further by A.Myrick Freeman III in 'Income Distribution and Planning for Public Investment', *American Economic Review*, June 1967.

50 This particular point was made recently with respect to railways in the Argentine. Cf. *A Long Range Transport Plan for Argentina*, Ministry of Public Works and Services, Transport Planning Group, Buenos Aires, 1962.

51 pp. 25–6, above.

52 E.g., *Transport Policy*, Comnd. 3057.

53 E.g., if it is desired to forbid some activity *completely*, legal prohibition is more sensible than a system of fines or charges.

54 E.g., delays due to imperfect liaison between different ministries or different departments of the same ministry.

55 I.e., assuming the total stock of vehicles using a given area to be divided between two firms.

56 This diagram and the succeeding one are a cross between those used by R.Turvey, 'On Divergences between Social Cost and Private Cost', *Economica*, August 1963, and that used in a different context by Richard A.Musgrave, *Theory of Public Finance*, McGraw-Hill, New York, 1959, p. 114.

57 *Op. cit.*, p. 310.

58 There may be further complications depending on which other taxes are reduced, or expenditures, increased, as a result of the tax.

59 Cf. J.H.Moore, *op. cit.*

3 Practices v. Principles

Introduction

Whereas chapter 2 was entirely concerned with general principles this chapter will be more devoted to practical considerations. We shall survey the charging practices and then the general financial position of public transport authorities in selected developing countries. We then consider the principal divergences between what we find in practice and what we might have expected on the basis of chapter 2. Subsequently, we explore the reasons for these divergences and try to assess their validity. Three appendices give more detailed factual information.

The general need for some survey of this sort before coming to specific suggestions on policy is self-evident. It would be quite wrong to suggest policies purely on the basis of chapter 2, without reference to institutional backgrounds. Conversely, a survey of such backgrounds needs to be conducted against the framework of principles set out in the preceding chapter.

It must be reiterated that we are confining ourselves in the main to a small number of countries – Nigeria, Uganda, Kenya, India – though isolated examples will be drawn from other countries when particularly relevant. We do not pretend that all our arguments apply to all our countries, let alone to others.

Furthermore, we shall, by and large, confine ourselves to road and rail transport. It might be asked how this picture should be modified once air and water transport are brought into the picture. One or two illustrations may suffice. In Nigeria, a special study put total ton-mileage of goods by rail and road in 1962 at some 3,200 millions, whereas that by water was estimated as 125 millions. The latter leaves out canoe traffic, but as the former leaves out head-loading, bicycle carriage, etc., the *ratio* may not be misleading. If one looks at passenger traffic data, one finds a figure of over 3,600 million passenger miles by road and rail in 1962 and only 15 million for air; correction for small-scale activity would tend to widen this margin. As another illustration, recent data for India[1] show the share of all transport other than road and rail (i.e., coastal and inland shipping, air, pipelines and motorways) to be 15·7 per cent of all traffic tonnage in India in 1962–3. On a ton-mileage basis, this ratio would probably be less because of the dominance of the Indian Railways in long distance haulage – though it should be added, aggregate data conceal very large regional differences. The relative unimportance of internal air travel at present also emerges from this report.[2]

It would seem, therefore, that in discussing present transport facilities in these countries one is covering the great bulk by concentrating largely on road and rail. We shall pursue this line of approach but with side references to air and water transport in cases where they are especially important or interesting.

Finally, we must emphasise now what will soon become very obvious: that the data available leave an enormous amount to be desired in both quantity and quality. This reservation must not be forgotten for one second throughout the ensuing pages.

Public Sector Transport Prices and Charges

Rail charges
The traditional basis of rail charges for goods in *Nigeria* both in the pre-1955 era when the railways were a government

department and more latterly during the régime of the Nigerian Railway Corporation has been that of charging what the traffic bear – or at any rate, that of not charging what the traffic will not bear. The tariff has sixteen classes, the basis of classification being essentially that of value. Historically, this has meant higher rates per ton-mile for imported manufactures than for some exported raw materials and foodstuffs. Though there are tapering provisions in the tariff for longer journeys, there is no evidence that these are closely bound up with cost variations. Variations in the ratio of price to direct (i.e., attributed average) costs are very substantial, e.g., price was 46 per cent of direct costs in the case of pigs but 326 per cent in the case of columbite in the late 1950s.[3] Too much weight should not be put on these comparisons as they involve some fairly arbitrary assumptions about cost allocation; they are no more than a broad indicator.

Various estimates[4] have been made of the costs and prices of road transport and they have usually come out with a range of about 5d–10d per ton-mile (for the late 1950s).[5] On the basis of these findings, a very rough generalisation would seem to be that road-haulage has cost advantages over rail for distances shorter than some 200–300 miles, and perhaps even greater distances in the case of trailers. For long hauls (e.g., the 700 miles from Kano to Lagos) the railway has definite advantages though this has not prevented serious competition in recent years from road hauliers for the transportation of the groundnut crop. There appear to be a number of explanations for this – e.g., rail charging policy, limitations of railway capacity at some times in some years, attempts to favour Northern Region road entrepreneurs for either economic or political reasons, etc.

In the case of passenger traffic, there is no taper, though it would appear that there are substantial savings in costs per passenger mile for long hauls.[6] As one might expect, lorry and bus operating costs are such that they can undercut the railway for short journeys but not for long ones.[7] There is no clearcut evidence about whether passenger services are profitable at the margin but the Stanford study, for instance, took the view that the financial position would be worse if all passenger services were discontinued, but, on the other hand, a later official study seemed to indicate the opposite.[8]

Although both the Nigerian Railway Corporation and the Federal government have in recent years made noises in the direction of altering rail tariffs on to a cost basis,[9] nothing much seems to have happened so far. This is hardly surprising when it is remembered that the present tariffs have been in existence for a long time, that there is acute scarcity of personnel for costing studies, that there have been a number of major changes in top management in recent years and that the railway was traditionally regarded primarily as an instrument for government purposes rather than a fully commercial enterprise.[10]

Outwardly, the charging system of *East African* Railways[11] has some standard characteristics – obligations to be a public carrier, to publish rates and not to show undue preferences, and so on. In addition, there has been an element of taper in rates charged; there have been special concessions in respect of Uganda; and the organisation has always been enjoined to assist agricultural, mining and industrial development so long as this was consistent with principles of prudent finance.[12] The result has been very considerable differences in average revenue per ton-mile, e.g., in 1964 for classes 1–4 of the tariff the figure was 34·4 cents and for class 10 (the lowest normal class) it was 14·7 cents.[13]

It has traditionally been assumed that high-rated goods were carried at prices above costs and that these subsidised the low-rated goods, but latterly, with the development of costing studies, some doubt has been shed on this argument.[14] It would appear, for instance, that although people thought that one effect of the existing rail tariff was to subsidise exports, there is not much evidence that this is the overall result – by and large rates on exports as a whole just about matched costs, though there were some commodities above and some below the line. Similarly, the taper as it has actually operated has favoured long-distance, but not medium-distance, traffic relatively to the

54

charges applicable if a cost-based taper were introduced. So the kind of cross-subsidisation which one actually finds in practice may well be different from that which was traditionally thought to exist.

An official publication on tariff policy in 1964[15] affirmed the general intention to move to a cost-based tariff especially by taking more account of the high costs of handling 'smalls' traffic and the higher proportionate terminal costs of handling short-distance traffic. However, the day when a full-blown cost-based tariff is in operation would appear to be still some way off.

It is usually argued that revenue from railway passengers in East Africa covers only two-thirds of the direct costs attributed to them. Whether this is so or not, there has unquestionably been a great deal of competition from road passenger transport in recent years. But passenger revenue is in any case a very small proportion of total revenue.

Railways in *India* have long based their freight rates on traditional value of service principles. Prasad[16] argues that the Indian Railways Act of 1890 was modelled on the British Railway and Canal Traffic Act of 1888, but without the crucial requirement that the treatment of home and foreign goods should be non-discriminating. Whatever the origins, the traditional policy was to favour exports of raw materials and imports of manufactures. This was brought out very clearly by a legal case in 1937; the railways were accused of charging higher freight rates on bunker coal to Calcutta than on coal for exports, but were expressly exonerated on the grounds that there was no obligation on them to charge the same rate for different cargoes of the same commodity. However, there have been a number of changes in the rate structure in recent years and some progress has been made towards reducing disparities.[17] But one could hardly claim that this is much more than a start, especially when the traditional telescoping of the rate structure with respect to distance is taken into account.

There are obvious obligations resting on Indian Railways

which have a familiar ring about them, e.g., those of a common carrier, the operation of unremunerative branch lines, special freight concessions, and so on. There are also, as in many other countries, enormous differences among the various parts of the system, with something like 58 per cent of the traffic being carried on 15 per cent of the route mileage.[18]

As in other countries, Indian Railways have suffered from road competition in recent years, with high-rated traffic hardly growing in size and actually falling as a percentage of the total. In a country of India's size, there are bound to be very large regional variations in costs per ton-mile for road transport and so comparisons with rail freight rates are extremely tricky. The most recent Report contents[19] itself with summarising the results of a special inquiry into road transport costs but a 1959 Report gave some figures which seemed to make the railways broadly competitive at that time.[20]

Indian rail passenger charges do not embody explicit discrimination in the same way as rail freight charges. They are fixed on a standard basis per passenger mile, but, of course, this implies that they do not vary between areas or between times of the day, the week, or the year, according to costs. On the basis of a somewhat arbitrary split of the common costs of track maintenance, signalling, etc. between passenger and freight it would appear that there is a general subsidy of passenger traffic by freight traffic.[21] There is also some reason to believe that first and third classes are more leniently treated than others and that suburban fares are subsidised.

Some broad generalisations may be made about the present position of railways in these various countries.[22] In the cases examined, the traditional pattern of railway rate-making has come under pressure in recent years. The single most important reason is clearly the growth of road freight transport which has been free of many of the limitations imposed on railways (e.g., common carrier, need to publish rates, etc.) and has been able to pick and choose among the traffic. Similarly, road passenger transport has made inroads. Other factors have also contributed to the railways' difficulties. One is the changing composition of goods traffic in a direction unfavourable to railways. Another is the need for a publicly owned organisation to set high standards of wages, fringe benefits, etc. This is a well-known phenomenon in European countries and has been seized on as an important point in Nigeria.[23] A closely related point is the obligation to take on unnecessary workers – or at the very least the impossibility of dismissing surplus labour – on grounds of national employment policy. Another problem which particularly afflicts large organisations is staff dishonesty and/or inefficiency. One example is Nigeria,[24] especially since the reduction in the number of expatriate staff; another is India.[25]

For all these various reasons, railways in the countries concerned are facing major readjustment problems.

Road charges, duties, etc.
We shall now look at the position of a few countries in some detail. Partial information on a wider range of countries is given in appendices 3A and 3B.

Before examining the system in any individual country, there is one general point of principle. In many countries, import duties on vehicles, vehicle parts and motor fuel play an important role; excise duties on such items are also to be found in some countries. It is obviously difficult to generalise about elasticities of demand and supply in these cases and to maintain with certainty that all such duties fall on road users. However, we do have some evidence in respect of duties on fuel oil, the most important single ingredient of this total. Appendix 3B, table 3·B2, shows that if one compares coastal locations in the ex-British African territories (e.g. ,Tanzania, Sierra Leone, Gambia, Nigeria) there was in 1966 a reasonably close correlation between the rate of tax and retail prices including tax. In other words, the evidence is that the oil companies tend to pass on local taxes to consumers and do not absorb them themselves – contrary to what is sometimes suggested.[26]

In the light of this, we shall assume that all such import duties do fall on road users. This is admittedly a large assumption but it at least has the merit of putting an upper limit to the estimates, in that if part of the duty is in fact borne by foreign suppliers we are over-estimating the contribution of road users. Finally, the same assumption in respect of excise duties may mean an over-estimate in respect of those directly concerned with road usage and an under-estimate in respect of those indirectly concerned.

In *Nigeria*, the main types of road revenue are three. First, Federal import duties ranging (in 1966) from 10 per cent on buses to a normal level of 33⅓ per cent on most vehicles, but reaching up to 150 per cent on the largest cars, were bringing in about £7m or some 30 per cent of the total in 1964–5. Second, there is a Federal tax on motor fuels; this is distributed to the Regions which may, in turn, clap on an extra tax (e.g., this is the practice in the Eastern Region). The total of petrol and diesel oil taxes was about £12m in 1964–5.[27] Finally, Regional government licencing of vehicles and drivers brought in some £4m in 1964–5. The main features were charges varying according to vehicle weight, rising to a maximum of £117 annual charge for the heaviest trucks; omnibuses were taxed at £20 per annum. The rates are the same in all Regions but nevertheless there have been considerable overall differences between Regions in these matters, the Eastern Region being well off and the Federal government badly off in relation to current outgoings on road construction and maintenance. As can be seen from the appendices, Nigerian vehicle import duties were at much the same levels as those in other African countries but the duty on gasoline (though not diesel fuel) was a bit less than in many other countries in 1966.

During the era of the East African Common Services Organisation (EACSO) there have been a number of road charges common to *Kenya*, *Uganda* and *Tanzania*. We shall say something about these common elements first and then supplement this later with some individual country details in respect of Kenya and Uganda.

Initially, the main features of the 'common market' administered by EACSO were:

1. A common external tariff (with slight local variations) and an internal free trade area for imported goods and local manufactures (but not local agricultural products).
2. An essentially common income tax system and common rates of excise taxes.
3. A common monetary and financial system with no restriction on inter-territorial movements of funds.

It is too early yet to assess all the implications of the East Africa Cooperation Treaty signed in June 1967 (e.g., the effects of the new 'transfer tax' on the freedom of inter-territorial trade) but it seems fair to say that the powers of individual territories to vary road-user charges independently of one another are less limited than they were. One particular example is that none of the three territories now allows vehicles from the others to operate inside it without levying an additional licence or licence-type charge.

The main features of the common external tariff on vehicles, etc. were in 1966 a duty of 30 per cent on many items, but with possibilities of higher levies (up to 50 per cent) on large-size cars and lower rates on lorries and buses (21 per cent) and on parts for local assembly (15 per cent). It should be noted, however, that the basic rate of 30 per cent applies to parts imported other than for assembly purposes. This latter point aroused criticism in the International Bank Report on Uganda,[28] on the grounds that such a high rate of duty encouraged the importing of inferior parts and also thefts of parts from vehicles.

There have been substantial changes in the rates of import duty in recent years. Before 1959 commercial vehicles were exempted from import duty; and there have also been big increases in other duties, e.g., whereas the effective rate of tax on gasoline from 1964 to 1966 was 1·85 shillings per imperial gallon, it was only 0·75 shillings per gallon in 1958. At the prices ruling for Shell products in Kampala in March 1966, the duty was

Table 3·1   Kenya Road Taxes etc., 1961–2 – 1964–5 (£m)

Year	Import duties	Purchase tax	Licences	Total
1961–2	4·9	nil	0·8	5·7
1962–3	6·1	neg.	0·8	6·9
1963–4	6·7	0·1	0·7	7·5
1964–5	7·1	0·2	0·8	8·1

Sources: Kenya Road Authority, *Annual Reports*; Kenya *Appropriation Accounts*; Statistical Department, EACSO

Notes: 1. Import duty revenue from bicycles and parts, all tyres and tubes and lubricating oils, etc. excluded. They would add about £0·5m to the 1964-5 total.
2. Some small local taxes are omitted but they are believed to be insignificant.
3. See note 31 p. 101 for method of adjusting EACSO data.

equivalent to an 80 per cent tax on the c.i.f. value in the case of diesel and a 65 per cent tax in the case of regular grade gasoline.

In *Kenya*, there are vehicle and drivers' licences revenues to take into account, as well as the items common to all three territories.[29] Licencing charges rise to 200s per annum for vehicles not exceeding 2,500 lb tare weight, with an extra 20s for each additional 250 lb or part thereof. Furthermore, there is also a flat £10 purchase tax levied on each transaction in secondhand vehicles. In 1964–5, total revenue from all taxes, etc. on road users was £8·1 m as shown in table 3·1 above.

It can be seen that import duties are much the most important constituent of the total; and then it might be added that duties on motor fuel amounted to over 75 per cent of this total in 1964–5. There has also been a substantial growth in the revenue total in recent years.

In *Uganda*, the import duties on vehicles and motor fuels are supplemented by a system of licence fees for vehicles (ranging from 50s per annum for a motor cycle to 900s for a 3-ton truck) and by driving licence fees.[30] The overall position is that in 1964–5 total revenue from road charges, etc. was £4·8m.[31] Of this total, some £4m came from import duties on vehicles, etc.

Table 3·2 Uganda Road Taxes, etc., 1950–65 (£m)

Year	Duties	Licences	Total
1950	0·47	0·06	0·5
1956–7	1·0	0·2	1·2
1962–3	2·9	0·6	3·5
1964–5	4·0	0·8	4·8

Source: E.K. Hawkins, *Road and Rail Transportation in an Underdeveloped Country (Uganda)*, H M S O, London, 1962; *Uganda Statistical Abstract, 1965*; and special information.

Note: Duties on bicycles and parts and on all tyres and tubes and lubricating oils are excluded from the above; they would add some £0·3m to the 1964–5 total.

Table 3·3 Ethiopia Road Taxes, etc., 1961–2 – 1964–5 (E$m)

Year	Import and Excise Duties		Licences	Total
	Vehicles and parts	Fuel		
1961–2	6·8	17·3	0·4	24·6
1962–3	7·1	19·1	1·0	27·2
1963–4	9·3	20·3	1·0	30·6
1964–5	9·1	22·6	1·1	32·8

Source: Informal estimates supplied in Ethiopia.

and fuel (the latter being responsible for nearly three-quarters of the total) and £0·8m from the various sorts of licences.

The growth of revenue from these sources, partly due to increases in tax rates and partly due to the growth of the tax base, can be seen from table 3·2 above. It is not surprising that, in view of these trends, road user revenues grew from something like 6 per cent of total government revenue in 1956–7 to 16 per cent in 1964–5.

Data for *Ethiopia* are thin, but they do seem to show a somewhat different pattern from other countries (see table 3·3 above. Licence fees, etc. play a very small part in the system and fuel taxes are an even larger share than usual of total import duties. Perhaps the most interesting feature is something not in the table. Since 1958 there has been a system whereby the Imperial Highway Authority has had contributions from local communities towards the development of feeder roads. In principle, the contribution can be in cash or in labour and materials, but the former is more normal since the best time for road building is also harvest time, when labour is not readily available. Contributions are supposed to be of the order of 75 per cent of total expenditure but in practice tend to be a good deal less. Nevertheless, some E$8m has been raised in this way over the years 1961–6. It is also proposed that local sources should be responsible for meeting the maintenance costs of work organised under this programme.

Charges on road users in *India* take a variety of forms. First, the central government levies customs duties on imported vehicles and tyres together with excise duties on both imported and home-produced vehicles, etc. The level of tariffs can be seen from appendix 3A; the excise duties were in 1966 around 12 per cent to 20 per cent for most vehicles. Second, there are three taxes on motor fuel – central government import duty, central excise tax and state sales taxes. Thirdly, there are state licencing charges for vehicles and drivers, etc. Fourth, a number of authorities levy extra duties at their frontiers. Fifth, there are taxes on passengers and goods.

We shall not try to list all these taxes in detail. From a revenue point of view the motor fuel taxes (55 per cent of the total in 1961–2) and the import and excise duties on vehicles and parts (22 per cent) are the most important. State taxes on buses and trucks vary considerably and so do the passenger taxes (usually a percentage of fares paid) and the goods taxes.[32] Even though the central import and excise duties are among the highest in the countries for which we have data, it would seem that the state taxes (other than the sales tax on motor fuel) are by far the greatest cause of trouble. Not only is the administration clumsy (e.g., separate operations in collecting the licencing duties and

Table 3·4 Nigerian Railway Finances (selected years) (£m

Year	Operating revenue	Operating expenses	Net operating income	
1949–50	5·9	5·1	0·8	
1958–9	15·8	13·7	2·0	1·1
1963–4	16·3	14·3	1·9	0·03
1964–5	14·2	15·6	−1·4	−3·4
1965–6	14·6	16·5	−1·9	−4·2

Source: *Nigerian Railway Corporation, Annual Reports.*

the passenger and goods taxes) but what is even worse is the liability of many vehicles to double taxation if they cross state frontiers. This has resulted in the astonishing phenomenon of the growth of trans-shipment areas at frontiers, to avoid the penalty of double taxation. Although the evils of this system have been recognised for a long time, very little seems to have been done so far to eliminate them.[33]

Public Sector Transport Finances

Rail finances

Table 3·4 above. shows the position in *Nigeria* for selected years, further details being given in appendix 3C. Up to 1959 the railways typically had an excess of revenue over operating expenses (including depreciation of some £2m per annum) and after debiting interest and tax charges and crediting investment income there was usually some surplus. Since 1959, there have been years in which net operating income was negative, and only one (1963–4) in which there was a small surplus after meeting interest payments (net of receipts). The situation has clearly deteriorated markedly in recent years, partly, though not exclusively, due to the opening of the Bornu extension. It has been necessary to raise new loans from the Federal government and there is now a substantial amount of accrued unpaid interest.[34]

Table 3·5 East African Railway Finances (selected years) (£m)

Year	Railway Revenue	Railway working expenditure	Railway renewals contributions	Railway loan charges	Balance
1955	17·5	12·9	1·6	1·5	+1·5
1959	19·5	13·9	2·0	2·9	+0·7
1963	21·0	15·6	2·0	3·7	−0·3
1964	21·6	16·2	2·1	4·0	−0·7
1965	23·0	16·7	2·1	4·4	−0·2

Source: *Kenya Statistical Abstracts.*

Note: A small amount of non-railway operations (road and water transport and hotel services) is included in the figures, but some small miscellaneous expenditures are omitted.

In *East Africa*, the financial position of the railways in recent years is summarised in table 3·5 above, further details being given in appendix 3C.

Despite the increases in railway revenues in recent years (increases from goods traffic more than offsetting reductions from passenger receipts) there has been a tendency for the total of all expenditures to outstrip revenue. The significance of these figures depends on the adequacy of the sums put aside for renewals of capital equipment. There was a major change in the method of computing these in 1957, but if we confine ourselves to the subsequent years, there has only been a small increase in annual contributions. It might be noted that the 1964 *Annual Report* expressed some apprehension about this figure but argued that the financial position of the railways did not permit an increase in the allocation. A consequence of the deterioration in the overall position is that it has not been possible to make any allocation for 'betterment' (i.e., improvement of capital equipment) in recent years. It is also expected that loan charges will increase in the years ahead, partly because of the time pattern of repayments and partly because higher interest rates will have to be paid on new loans or conversions.[35]

In *India*, the first essential of railway finances is to make an annual contribution, prescribed in advance, to a Depreciation Reserve Fund – in 1964–5 the sum required was 800 million rupees, with considerable increases foreshadowed in the years ahead. Second, from 1964–5 an annual contribution to a Pension Fund (120 million rupees in 1964–5) has to be made. Third, an annual dividend has to be paid into the general revenues of government at predetermined rates (the maximum being now 6 per cent) on the effective capital-at-charge. Fourth, a payment was until recently made to state governments in lieu of a former tax on passenger fares. The precise details of the last two payments are complicated but the approximate figure for 1964–5 was about 1,000 million rupees with the prospect of a somewhat higher figure in later years. Finally, the net annual surpluses remaining, if any, are credited to a Development Fund.

In the late 1950s contributions to the Depreciation and Development Funds were insufficient to meet the demands on them though the situation improved subsequently.

Net earnings (i.e., after depreciation but before payment of dividends) seem to have been on an upward trend over the last few years, rising from 503 million rupees in 1955–6 to 1,181 million in 1964–5, but with marked annual fluctuations. The conclusion of the *Committee on Transport Policy* was:[36]

The broad conclusion which emerges from this analysis is that although the railways have been showing surpluses from year to year, in some recent years they have had difficulty in meeting commitments towards the Development Fund and the Depreciation Reserve Fund out of their current earnings and were obliged to draw either on the balances in the Funds accumulated in the past or on loans from General Revenues. The railways obviously will have to be prepared to meet heavier financial commitments in future years.

Road finances
In principle, estimates of the public financial operations of roads should be on the basis of current costs of maintenance plus interest and depreciation on capital appropriately defined;[37] but

frequently lack of data drives one to comparisons of revenue from road users with the total of maintenance and capital expenditure in a given year. With a given stock of capital and constant prices, the two methods would give the same answers; but with a rapidly growing stock of roads in the countries which interest us, one would expect the second measure to be a more severe test for surpluses; and the severity will be enhanced if interest costs are excluded, or only partially included.

In *Nigeria*, the Stanford Research Institute enquiry[38] bravely attempted the task of estimating the equation between road user charges and costs on both bases. They found that in 1959 both methods gave an excess of expenditure over revenue, but as might be expected the excess was considerably greater when expenditure is based on current investment plus maintenance.[39] However, in view of the inevitable statistical limitations of the exercise it would not be wise to put much weight on it.

It is worth noting that another calculation in respect of the Western Region only and for the period 1955–60, shows total revenue from road users of £7·9m and expenditure of £8·6m.[40]

More recent figures[41] show Federal plus Regional (but excluding local) expenditure, current plus capital, running at something like £10m – £12m per annum, reaching a peak of £13m in 1964–5. Road-user charges (Federal import duties on vehicles, etc. and duties on motor fuels plus Regional licencing taxes on vehicles and drivers) have been substantially more, e.g., £24m in 1964–5. This suggests a surplus measured on this crude basis. But it should be noted that there are considerable Regional variations hidden by these overall data; and as projections of capital expenditures in the next few years showed large increases the surplus was expected to diminish rapidly.

In the case of *Uganda*, total revenue from road users in the form of import duties, fuel taxes and licences was £4·8m in 1964–5 (£4m in 1963–4),[42] whereas all government road expenditure, capital plus current, was of the order of £2m – 3m in both years. Whereas the pattern in the late 1950s was of a substantial deficit calculated on this basis, the surplus has grown steadily in the last few years.

Hawkins[43] estimated that the replacement value of Uganda roads could be put at £32m in 1956–7. Taking an interest rate of 5 per cent and adding in £0·7m for annual maintenance costs gave him a total of £2·3m, whereas revenue at that time was only £1·2m. Very roughly, it would appear that if this calculation were extended to make it more or less up to date one would get an annual expenditure figure of around £3m – which still leaves current revenue showing a surplus.

In *Kenya*, road user tax revenues rose rapidly in the 1960s from £5·7m in 1961–2 to £7·5m in 1963–4 and £8·1m in 1964–5.[44] As total expenditure, recurrent plus non-recurrent, in the latter year was about £3·3m this would seem to indicate a substantial 'surplus'. However, expenditure seemed likely to rise sharply in 1965–6, quite apart from the inherent weaknesses of this method of comparison.

In *Ethiopia*, the responsibility for the main road expenditure (and to a limited extent on certain municipal secondary and provincial roads) rests with a special organisation, the Imperial Highway Authority. The latest available data show that in 1961–2 total user charges were E$24·6m and total expenditure (capital plus current) E$24·2m; and in 1962–3 E$27·2m and E$25·2m respectively. Too much emphasis should not be placed on this data as local taxes on road users and local expenditure are omitted (except insofar as some of the Authority's expenditure is in the form of grants towards the latter). But so far as the figures go, they give a similar impression to those for the other African countries examined.[45]

In *India*, the latest available data[46] show total revenue (central import and excise duties, state motor vehicle taxes, sales taxes on fuel and passenger goods taxes) as 1,940 million rupees in 1961–2 and total expenditure (development plus maintenance) as 1,183 million rupees, thereby yielding a surplus of 757 million rupees. This pattern has prevailed for a number of years with a steady tendency for the annual surplus to rise (e.g., it was not more than about 500 million rupees in 1953–4).[47] We also had an estimate a few years ago by the capital stock method. The Motor Vehicle Taxation Enquiry Committee[48] estimated that in 1949 road-user tax, etc., receipts in the Pt. A states[49] was 233 million rupees whereas total outgoings could be put at 147 million rupees (30 million rupees capital charges, on the basis of a 4 per cent charge on a capital stock of 750 million rupees *plus* 117 million rupees maintenance expenditure). This can be compared with an estimate given in the same Report of actual expenditure on capital projects and maintenance of 177 million rupees – indicating a surplus of 56 million rupees (compared to 86 million on the first basis).[50]

In the case of India, one must also mention the state transport undertakings,[51] which carry passengers in some twelve states. The last available data show that total revenue was 742 million rupees in 1960–1 and total operating costs 659 million rupees, giving a national surplus of 83. It is not known, however, what sort of allowance has been made for interest and depreciation in these figures.

Road transport restrictions
We must now devote a little space to road transport restrictions. The form taken by these restrictions varies considerably from one country to another. In some ways, the restrictions are (on paper, at any rate) more severe in India that in the other countries we are examining.[52] The operation of commercial motor transport has been regulated for a number of years by a series of Acts involving both Union and state governments. Essentially, the system is that commercial motor transport, whether for goods or passenger carriage, cannot operate without a permit specifying area and manner of operation and possibly also rates, schedules, etc. The present situation seems to be that, although delays may be encountered, permits to operate can usually be obtained, there being no upper limit to their number. The nature of the permit may leave something to be desired, however. First, it may be of a temporary nature only; second, there seems to

have been some discrimination against particular types of vehicles, especially semi-trailers; third, there may be severe restrictions on route or distance of operation. The latter is particularly so when inter-state operations are involved and there have been many complaints over the years of the frustration and wastes involved where trans-shipments have been necessary at state frontiers because of licencing restrictions.[53] The usual conclusion is that the legislation has been both an instrument for regulating competition within the road industry and one for affecting the relative roles of road and rail transportation.

At the other end of the spectrum, there have been some attempts to restrict road vehicle operations in *Nigeria*. For instance, vehicle taxes were doubled on some roads in the 1930s to protect the railways' interests.[54] And for many years there has been legislation on the statute book regulating competition in both goods and passenger carriage.[55] To date, however, there has been no move to apply these regulations, despite recommendations pointing in this direction.

East African countries tend to lie between these two extremes. There have been restrictions on both freight and road operations in *Kenya* ever since 1932. The major consideration for freight at any rate has always been the protection of railway interests, e.g., the general principle (subject to specific exceptions) is that where adequate railway services exist, licences are not normally issued for more than thirty miles. In *Uganda*, there are no restrictions on the goods side but sections of the road passenger market have been subject to a restrictive licencing system since pre-war days. In the case of omnibus licencing, the regulations seem to have been imposed in such a way as to favour existing or potential large undertakings – partly by insisting on top quality buses (beyond the means of small operators) and partly by imposing discriminatory conditions in favour of large operators.[56]

The relevance of this very important subject to our present discussion is that the overall financial aspects of public rail and

69

road facilities in each country have to be seen against this background. Insofar as regulation of road vehicles or road operation has slowed down the growth of road transport, this is likely to mean that rail revenues have been greater and receipts from vehicle licencing, fuel duties and so on less than would otherwise have been the case. The differential impetus given to the various types of road transport may also have had some effect on total road revenues, though that is more difficult to establish. At the same time, we should note that all the railways in the countries considered have had their ups and downs, despite the very differing types and degrees of road restrictions. It is not the case, for instance, that Indian Railways have been uniformly prosperous and Nigerian Railways always in the red. So this suggests that, although restrictions on road usage are of some relevance in this context, they do not swamp all other considerations.

Contrasts Between Theory and Practice

Chapter 2 set out the general principles on which public transport pricing policies should be conducted and the circumstances under which deficits might be justified. In this chapter we have tried to sketch some of the pricing practices actually prevailing in developing countries and the financial position in which railways, etc. typically find themselves. We must now look at the contrasts between what one might hope to find on theoretical grounds and what is actually found in practice. It must be emphasised from the beginning that we shall draw on our background knowledge of public enterprise practices in these countries as well as on the statistical material presented above.

In general principle, we should, on the basis of chapter 2, hope to find that transport charges bear some definable relationship to marginal costs, so that charges for one mode, one distance or one commodity as against another are related on this basis – always subject to explicit and specific adjustments to allow for externalities, income distribution and the like. But it will be readily appreciated from our survey above that such principles are not in fact carried through into practical methods of charging. The standard system in the railways examined was to charge on a value of service basis, with a great deal of cross-subsidisation between freight and passenger traffic, between suburban passengers and others, between low-value and high-value goods, between short and long distances, between goods destined for or emanating from other countries and those of a purely domestic character – and so on. Cross-subsidisation is clearly not ruled out as a matter of principle, in that there are circumstances in which some services should be run at a profit and some at a loss, but there is no evidence to show that the cross-subsidisation justifiable on theoretical grounds is the kind found in practice. As for road charging, it is clear that import duties and fuel taxes have been imposed as relatively easy and simple ways of raising revenue without any regard to the appropriate relative charges in urban and rural areas, the problems of congestion costs in large towns at peak hours, the differing costs of providing roads capable of bearing light and heavy vehicles, and so on.

Nor does one feel much more confidence if one looks at ways of accounting for capital costs. In principle, one needs to take cognisance of replacement costs of capital equipment which has to be renewed, and of alternative use values of non-renewable assets. But we do not find such procedures in practice. With regard to interest rates, one needs a figure which makes any necessary allowances for social (as distinct from private) time preference, for the opportunity cost of diverting capital from private to public enterprise, for risk and uncertainty, for capital market imperfections (necessitating reliance on internal financing), and so on.[57] Once again, such ideas are not exactly common in actual pricing practices.

So the first impressions from a perusal of the evidence must be that of wide divergences between theory and practice. In this case, first impressions are almost certainly correct but it is at the same time necessary to mention some possible qualifications. Disentangling the many elements of jointness and allowing for the many discontinuities in transport costs is notoriously difficult. After all, the amount of progress to date in many advanced countries in these matters is pretty small. Quite apart from such intrinsic and inherent difficulties, the simple fact is that there have been very few attempts to investigate costs on any thoroughgoing basis in the countries which concern us. Even with Indian Railways, a large organisation established for many years, it is possible for a recent writer to come to the following conclusion:

The railways have for many years attempted to compute some ill-defined concept of fully distributed average cost based on non-statistical cost accounting methods and have never seriously attempted to compute marginal costs.[58]

It is no doubt possible to make even stronger indictments in other cases.

But if, in fact, there is very little knowledge of costs, especially marginal costs, we cannot be completely certain that methods of charging which are allegedly based on value of service or similar principles do not correspond to a costs basis. As mentioned already,[59] a recent investigation has demonstrated that the subsidy to exports which was thought to be a clear feature of the East Africa Railway tariff may not in fact exist at all. So long as detailed cost information is so scarce there must therefore be some elements of doubt about the extent to which charging practices do differ from the ideal. But it would clearly be completely accidental if they came very close to it; and most observers seem to conclude, albeit with due caution, that substantial divergences do in fact exist between relative prices and relative costs on both road and rail.[60]

It became evident in chapter 1 that there were some circumstances in which it was appropriate for public enterprises to run at a loss and some in which they should make large profits. We have seen in this chapter that in practice railways and roads exhibit a variety of different relationships between income and expenditure.[61] Is it at all possible to say whether the surpluses or deficits actually found correspond to those which are theoretically justifiable?

It would require a great deal more information than is available to give any categorical answer to this question. To begin with, the recorded data are obviously unsatisfactory or incomplete in a variety of ways. We have seen that in practice calculations of capital costs are on a historic rather than a replacement basis; and that interest rates used in public enterprise accounts may or may not have any economic meaning. In the case of roads, it is only on some occasions that we have information to make calculations about current account (as distinct from a combination of current and capital account) operations; and when we do, there are all sorts of minor items such as costs of maintaining roads inside cities, road policing, costs of road accidents falling on government, and so on, which tend to be left out. So we must be very clear that the accounting data actually available are very deficient. But there is one straw in the wind. We saw earlier that in Uganda there has certainly been an excess of road revenues over the total of current plus capital expenditure in recent years, and possibly one over a rough figure of interest on road capital etc. However, the International Bank argued:[62]

On the basis of very rough calculations of our own, we feel sure that present revenues from special charges, in the sense that we have used the latter term, are at present insufficient to meet the road-users' share of real costs.

It should be emphasised that the theoretical arguments set out in chapter 2 for working at a surplus or loss were of a very general character. They clearly have to be tailored to the particular circumstances of particular countries before one can hope for an adequate answer. One must take account of a large number of particularised phenomena, such as the government's current and prospective budgetary position, the importance of externalities, the degree of competition in the economy, and so on. There may be many cases where some pricing feature is justifiable theoretically when all these complications have been considered, even though there appears to be a conflict at first sight.

However, it would seem extremely unlikely that even if we could estimate 'true' surpluses and deficits, these would correspond to those 'truly' justifiable in theoretical terms. It *may* be that rail or road charges happen to be particularly high for services which strain capacity; it *may* be that very low charges correspond to the situation where there would be a larger reduction in benefits than costs if capacity were curtailed; it *may* be that discriminatory pricing, when practised, is to be preferred to finance out of general government revenues. But it would be nothing short of miraculous if there were any such close correspondence between desirable and actual surpluses and deficits in all cases.

Reasons for Contrasts

There are a number of possible reasons for these contrasts between general principles and actual practices. First, it may be that the relevant administrators are wholly or partially ignorant of the principles set out in chapter 2. Second, it may be a matter of sheer inertia or conservatism. Third, even though the principles are known they may be thought to be irrelevant in the circumstances of developing countries. Fourth, even though they may be thought relevant, their practical applicability may be questioned. Fifth, even if none of the reasons above apply it may still be thought that the net economic gains from applying these principles are so unimportant that they are not worth worrying about. We shall now explore each of these arguments in turn under the headings of ignorance, inertia, irrelevance, inapplicability and unimportance.

74

Ignorance

We need not spend very much time on this point. On the one hand, the general principles of marginal cost pricing are widely known among economists and have been disseminated in the reports of countless consultants, advisers, missions and the like. On the other hand, it is only in recent years that these ideas have been developed in further (though by no means yet complete) detail and there are well-recognised lags in the process by which general theoretical principles filter into the consciousness of politicians or administrators. So even if one were to err on the generous side and assume that every person in a developing country with an economic training had fully assimilated these ideas, a long gestation period would still be likely before there were any serious attempts at application.

We do not pretend to be able to generalise on how far this digestion process has gone in developing countries. Anything like a proper appraisal would require far more resources than we had at our command. But arguing from the position in one advanced country, one must suppose that ignorance or at any rate incomplete knowledge of these principles at the relevant levels in the political and administrative hierarchy, is still an important consideration. And we have certainly not come across any evidence, oral or written, to refute this general impression. So the natural presumption is that this argument is important.

Inertia

Even if it were not a matter of simple ignorance, the divergence between principles and practices might simply be a reflection of sluggish administrations unwilling to move away from time-honoured practices. Clearly, there is something in this argument.[63] It is easy to make the mistake of thinking that one is dealing with new administrative structures when one has a lot of new governments. But this is simply not true in many cases: the pattern of government was largely set in ex-British Africa before 1914, and in the case of India it goes back much further. So it would be an enormous mistake to think that one is starting with a *tabula rasa*, or that the slothful delays of bureaucracy are not likely to arise and affect this area of administration as well as others.

Irrelevance

Even if governments of developing countries are cognisant of general pricing principles, and are able to implement them in a fully co-ordinated fashion (the latter is an important proviso, as we shall see), they may have a number of reservations about them. It might be argued, for instance, that imperfections of competition in goods and factor markets, or externalities, whether on the costs or the benefits side, in developing countries are so far-reaching that there is no particular reason why there should be a close alignment of prices and costs in public transport. This is the 'any old price will do' argument which one finds in some of the second-best discussions. As another example, it can be argued that, whether judged by the contribution transport is thought to have made to development in the nineteenth century or the contrasts between actual transport provision in developing and advanced countries today (e.g., in terms of road and rail mileage relative to area or population), the sky is the limit for such needs and all the nice refinements about whether public subsidies should be granted or not should be forgotten.

Many other examples of alleged irrelevance could be produced[64] but these are sufficient for our immediate purposes. Obviously, propositions of this sort raise issues which it is impossible to settle in a few words, and perhaps not even with many. But we have already laid the foundations of the relevant comments in chapter 2. We discussed there[65] the sorts of considerations which determine the extent of price/marginal cost divergences. Although it would be ridiculous to pretend that any developing country approximates to the textbook perfect competition model there are a number of factors making for competition which are not always given adequate weight (e.g., the importance of foreign trade in many economies, though India is an exception), the role played by small independent units of

76

production such as peasant cultivators, the pervasive nature of domestic trading, and so on. Similarly, we have also explored the arguments for subsidising public transport in the context of economic growth and found that it is easy to under-estimate the macro-economic importance of minimising budgetary deficits and to over-estimate (or double-count) the micro-economic significance of encouraging public transport facilities.[66]

The last thing one could claim is that such propositions do more than touch on this big subject. But our only need here is to demonstrate that the pricing principles outlined in chapter 2 are not wholly irrelevant to developing countries. Once this is established, the gap between theory and practice has to be explained in other ways.

We assumed above that governments speak with one voice when considering the relevance of general pricing principles. In reality, this is unlikely and it may well be the case that even though, say, a Finance Ministry understands the price-marginal cost arguments perfectly well, another arm of government thinks that its job is simply to maximise profits on its own operations. It has been argued, for instance,[67] that a major reason why Indian Railways have pursued their discriminatory rate policy has been their concentration on profit maximisation. The case is also cited[68] of the Rajasthan state government in India proposing to develop the Rajasthan Canal and yet simultaneously pressing for road and rail facilities parallel to it. We are not concerned with the ins and outs of these particular examples, but we simply make the point that acceptance of the pricing principles in chapter 2 has to percolate through all the relevant levels of government before they can be said to be fully accepted.

Inapplicability

Even if the standard pricing principles are not rejected on theoretical grounds, it may still be thought that they are politically or technically difficult to apply.

Political arguments of this sort are familiar in every country. Once a particular set of prices is established there are vested interests among consumers in seeing that these are not raised in an upward direction or that the standard or frequency of transport service is not reduced. This may take the form of defending the interests of particular modes of transport (e.g., railways) of particular groups (e.g., lowest class rail passenger fares in India) or particular areas (e.g., the arrangements in favour of Uganda in the East African Railways tariff structure and the decision of the Northern Nigerian Marketing Board to send groundnuts by road rather than by rail to Lagos, not on grounds of costs but because a larger proportion of the transport proceeds would then accrue to residents of the Northern Region). When, as often is the case, variations in rate structures can only be accomplished by a lengthy and public procedure, these political obstacles to change are likely to be even more marked.

At the technical level, there are many difficulties to overcome. We have already referred to the fact that there is a great deal of ignorance about the costs of particular transport operations, whether by road or rail, and that the technical personnel to make detailed cost calculations are thin on the ground. It is simply no good thinking that one can transform a railway tariff from a value of service basis to a cost basis overnight; or that one can in a matter of days produce a detailed assessment of the incremental costs of roads imposed by different types of vehicles. This is not meant to denigrate in any way the work currently going on in these fields but simply to emphasise that it is a slow business.

Even if costing personnel were more readily available there would be hard nuts to crack in the way of allocating common costs, especially in economies which are so poor that many transactions take place in small lots.[69] There are also many discontinuities to face on the demand side for transport. Many developing countries typically have bulky agricultural crops or raw materials being sent to the ports, with much less bulky manufactured imports to be conveyed in the other direction.[70] In addition, there may be marked seasonal variations in transport demands in agricultural countries,[71] and marked changes from one year to another depending on the variability of harvests under tropical conditions. On the other hand, low levels of income mean that there are not the same holiday or weekend transport peaks as in more advanced countries.

Nor, finally, can it be said that theoretically acceptable pricing policies are so common in advanced countries that the smallest tendency to a demonstration effect in this area would have ensured their adoption by developing countries.

Unimportance

Even if the general relevance of the principles is admitted and the practical objections to implementing them are not overwhelming, it may still be thought that the net benefits from implementation would be so small in relation to the costs of change-over as to be of no consequence.

Failure to adopt theoretically correct practices can, of course, be explained by the fact that the relevant authorities *believe* the benefits from doing so to be very small – quite irrespective of whether they are right or wrong in their beliefs. But it is of some moment to ask whether in fact there are grounds for thinking that the consequences of nonconformity are important.

As (more or less) every schoolboy knows, one cannot experiment in economics and nail down for certain what the situation would have been if transport charges, taxes, etc. had been different from what they were, but other things were kept unchanged. All we can do is to collect a number of necessarily incomplete fragments of evidence and try to form some judgment on the light they shed.

Arguments that public transport charges are of no real consequence are usually based on the proposition that the public element in transport costs is very small or that transport costs as a whole are small relative to total costs of production, distribution, etc.

On this kind of basis it has been argued, for instance, that a movement towards a cost-based tariff on East African Railways would not benefit traditional exports very much as the transport element in cost is small for most of them.[72] There is also some evidence to show that public charges, duties, etc. form a small proportion of total costs of conveyance by road. In Uganda in the late 1950s the various duties must have amounted to something like between 10 and 20 per cent of operating costs (including depreciation but not interest charges) of road hauliers.[73] Even though the percentage is likely to be higher today, the fact that such duties are still not a large proportion of total costs is clearly important for policy purposes. In the case of India, it can be estimated[74] that the duty element in total operating costs of road hauliers was also of the order of 10 to 20 per cent.

Another sort of reason why changes in transport prices might have little effect is that other changes, of an opposing character, could more or less automatically come into play. Marketing Boards have sometimes worked on the principle that they should organise produce buying prices so as to shield producers from differential transport costs.[75]

So if the different arms of government are not acting in complete union – a state of affairs not without precedent – one may easily find the effects of relative changes in transport charges counteracted in this manner.

We now turn to the evidence for the view that gaps between desirable and actual transport charges do matter. Obviously, one can make the general point about the need to utilise scarce capital resources as fully as possible in poor countries. But one must try to put more body than this into the argument.

One pair of authors[76] has argued that the discriminating nature of the Indian Railway tariff has had important effects on the location of industry e.g., low freight rates for coal have meant that new plants have not been under any necessity to locate themselves near coalfields, and also that the use of oil has not gone as far as it might have done. So for both those reasons there has been a greater strain on the transport system than was necessary. They conclude:

The rate structure obscures rather than reflects the real cost of transportation, encourages excessive movement, and results in no profits, with no indication of the type and size of capacity increases required to alleviate the evident scarcity.[77]

Carlin[78] has endorsed these conclusions and pointed to additional consequences of the traditional rate-fixing system – such as over-expansion of passenger traffic relative to freight, railway bottle-necks with consequent repercussions on industrial efficiency, over-investment in rail capacity, etc.

Two examples may be given of malpricing – or at any rate malpricing combined with administrative regulations – in respect of roads. It has been argued in the case of Uganda that insistence on omnibus operators buying high-quality, heavily-built vehicles and the refusal to allow joint carriage of freight and passengers has militated against the development of an indigenous road transport industry and, by pushing up costs, has hindered trading.[79] And in the case of India, the tax and licencing system has had the extraordinary consequences – already referred to but in need of continuing repetition – of the growth of trans-shipment areas at state frontiers with obvious consequences for costs of road transport.[80]

On a different plane, one can argue very strongly that it is important for public transport charging to make a sizeable contribution to government revenues – or at least that the contribution should not be negative. Most developing countries are in a position where they find raising revenues to meet the many and varied needs of education, health services, irrigation and so on a virtually impossible task already. If one is going to allow public transport deficits to arise as well one of two outcomes is likely. They may lead to larger budget deficits with inflationary consequences as in the (by now) classic cases of Brazil and Argentina. Alternatively, if deficits are met by more taxes these additional revenues are likely to come from additional indirect taxes, given the present administrative structure of revenue raising in most developing countries. It may prove possible to raise more revenue from luxury goods consumption in some cases but far more frequently reliance will have to be placed on excises on

81

items of mass consumption – with obvious unpalatable consequences in terms of political unpopularity, effects on income distribution, and so on.

Any conclusions about the importance of the divergences between theory and practice in transport pricing must be tentative. But, on balance, it does look as if some rather serious consequences, both at micro- and macro-levels, may result.

Summary

An account has been given of road and rail charging practices in selected countries, together with some rough assessments of the overall financial position of public transport services. We then drew some of the main contrasts which would appear to exist between actual practices and those deemed theoretically desirable on the basis of chapter 2. We have subsequently discussed the reasons for these contrasts and analysed their relative importance. With this behind us, we can now go forward to consider those improvements in arrangements which would appear to be feasible in the reasonably near future.

Appendix 3A
Road Vehicle Import Duty Rates

1. *Countries Covered*
Nigeria, Sierra Leone, Ghana, Gambia, West African Customs Union (Dahomey, Ivory Coast, Mauritania, Niger, Senegal, Upper Volta), Democratic Republic of the Congo, Zambia, Rhodesia, Malawi, Kenya, Uganda, Tanzania, Ethiopia, Algeria, Tunisia, Morocco, India, Pakistan, Ceylon, Turkey.

2. *Items Included*
Cars, omnibuses, trucks, motor cycles, bicycles, vehicle parts, tyres and tubes. Parts imported for the local assembly of vehicles are not included – frequently they carry a lower tax rate than that relating to the assembled imported vehicle.

3. *Basis of Duty*
The rates quoted are those believed to be current by the Board of Trade, London, in the second quarter of 1966.

In all cases except Zambia, Rhodesia, Malawi and Ethiopia, ad valorem rates are applied to c.i.f. price. In the case of Ethiopia it is c.i.f. price plus 1 per cent; in the case of the other three countries, f.o.b. price is used. The countries listed below have a preferential import duty system. Where this is the case, two rates are quoted in the table below to indicate the degree of preference conferred on the major exporter to the country concerned.

(a) Rhodesia, Malawi, Gambia, Pakistan, India, Ceylon – preference granted to British goods.

(b) Turkey – preference granted to GATT goods.

(c) West African Customs Union – preference granted to Franc Zone and other EEC countries.

(d) Algeria – France and EEC countries.

4. *Related Duties*
A number of countries charge additional taxes as well as import duties. These are listed below, the rates being shown there or else in footnotes to the main table. There is no guarantee that the list is

Table 3·A1 Current Import Duty Rates on Vehicles and Vehicle Parts in Selected Developing Countries (Second Quarter 1966)

Percentages except where otherwise stated

Country	Cars		Lorries		Buses		Car parts		Lorry parts		Bus parts	
Nigeria	33⅓–150[1]		33⅓		10		33⅓		33⅓		33⅓	
Sierra Leone	31¼–60[1]		21½		21½		25		25		25	
Ghana[2]	25		25		25		10		10		10	
Gambia[3]	30	15	30	15	30	15	30	15	30	15	30	15
West African Customs Union[4]	20	25	15	25	15	25	15	15	15	15	15	15
Congo (Kinshasa)	20		10		10		5		5		5	
Zambia	30–50[5]		10		10		10		10		10	
Rhodesia[6]	35–57½		20–25		20	10	c.30	c.20	c.30	c.20	c.30	c.20
		30–52½[5]		10–15[5]								
Malawi[6]	37½–47½		25	10	20	5	30	10	30	10	30	10
		15–25[5]										
Kenya	30–50[1]		25		25		30		30		30	
Uganda	30–50[1]		25		25		30		30		30	
Tanzania	30–50[1 7]		20		20		30		30		30	
Ethiopia[8]	20–40[9]		E$0·25 per Kg.		E$0·5 per Kg.		40		40		40	
Algeria[10]	32	17	31–33	16[1]	25–36	10–15[11]	nil		nil		nil	
Tunisia[12]	33		22		27½		11		11		11	
Morocco[13]	25–60	38–76[1]	32½	46	32½	46	15–30	27–43	15–30	27–43	15–30	27–43
India[14]	60		50		60	52½	60		42½		42½	
Pakistan[15]	25–250[5]		35		27½		Duty applicable to vehicle or 50 per cent					
Ceylon[16]	60– R5300+ 410%	52½– R4850+ 402½%	35	27½	35	27½	57½	50	57½	50	57½	50
	on excess over R6000											
Turkey[17]	75	25	60	25	75	25	50–75	10–25	50–75	10–25	50–75	10–25

Table 3·A1 Continued

Country	Tyres	Tubes	Motorcycles	Bicycles[18]	Motorcycle Parts	Bicycle Parts
Nigeria	0–33[19]	0–33	33⅓	33⅓	33⅓	33⅓
Sierra Leone	11	11	31¼–60[1]	11	25	25
Ghana[2]	50[20]	50[20]	15	15	10	15
Gambia[3]	30 15	30 15	30 15	30 15	30 15	30 15
West African Customs Union[4]	20 15–25[21]	20 15–25[21]	20 5	20 5	20 5	20 5
Congo (Kinshasa)	15	15[22]	20	15	5	5
Zambia	10	10	25	10	10	10
Rhodesia[6]	NA	NA	100 27–30	100+£1 35+£1	25 15	100 35
Malawi[6]	NA	NA	100 15	100 10	30 10	100 20
Kenya	1/25 shills. per lb.[23]	1/25 shills. per lb.[23]	30	30	30	30
Uganda	,, ,,	,, ,,	30	30	30	30
Tanzania	,, ,,	,, ,,	30	30	30	30
Ethiopia[8]	E$0·35 per Kg.[24]	E$0·25 per Kg.	20	15	40	15
Algeria[10]	15 8	15 8	10–15 3–5[1]	10 3	NA	NA
Tunisia[12]	11–22[21]	11–22[21]	22	16·5	NA	10
Morocco[13]	25–40 38–54[21]	40 54	25 38	20 32½	15 27	15–25 27–38
India[14]	50	50	60 52½	100 90	60 40	100 90
Pakistan[15]	50	50	25	50	40	50
Ceylon[16]	72 72[25]	72 72[25]	40 32½	33 23	57½ 50	33 23
Turkey[17]	40	40	60 40	50	20	20

PRACTICES V. PRINCIPLES

Notes

1 Rate increases with size of cubic-capacity of engine.

2 Additionally the following are subject to purchase tax (the rate increasing with the value of the vehicle): Cars, 20 per cent–100 per cent; commercial vehicles, 5 per cent–33⅓ per cent; motorcycles, 12½ per cent.

3 In each column are stated (in order) the general rate and preferential rate.

4 In each column are stated (in order) the fiscal duty and the customs duty. The former is payable by all countries. Franc Zone and EEC countries are exempted from the second. Certain countries (not including UK) are required to pay the customs duty at treble the rate specified.

5 Rate increase, with c.i.f. value.

6 Highest rate and UK rate quoted for each commodity.

7 Registration tax (on initial registration) also payable on private motor vehicles varying between 10 per cent and 20 per cent according to c.c. size of engine.

8 Additional duties of transaction tax and sales tax chargeable.

9 Increases with c.i.f. value and net weight of vehicle.

10 The UK rate and French rate are quoted in each column. In addition a production tax is chargeable – see details on p. 88.

11 Rate increases with seating capacity.

12 Production taxes, consumption taxes, consumption duties and National Defence Fund Taxes also payable as below:

    a. Private cars – consumption tax 29 per cent or 36 per cent (depending upon the employment of the importer), production tax of 18 per cent or 22½ per cent, consumption duty of D.132/vehicle plus National Defence Tax of 10 per cent of *both* consumption tax and consumption duty.

    b. Motorcycles and bicycles – consumption tax 18½ per cent or 23 per cent, production tax of 16½ per cent or 21 per cent plus National Defence Tax of 10 per cent of consumption tax.

    c. Tyres – consumption duty of 30–25 per cent, production tax of 18 per cent or 14 per cent, National Defence Tax of 10 per cent of consumption duty.

    d. All other items specified pay production tax of 18 per cent or 14 per cent.

13 The rate quoted in the left side of each column is the Working Tariff rate. The rate quoted in the right side of each column is the Working Tariff plus 2·5 per cent special tax, 1 per cent stamp duty, and 8 per cent transaction tax.

14 India operates a preferential tariff in favour of certain UK goods and these rates are shown in the right hand of the appropriate columns (even more favourable rates are afforded to Burma – these are not shown). In addition to the import duties shown, excise duties are payable on duty paid value as follows:

    a. Motorcars, 13 per cent–20 per cent (depending on engine power).

    b. Trucks and buses, 12 per cent–15 per cent (depending on engine power).

86

c. Motorcycles, 9 per cent.

d. Bicycles, R2 or R4 each.

e. Tyres, 18 per cent (except motorcycles 48 per cent).

15 Sales tax of 15 per cent of duty paid value plus defence surcharge of 25 per cent of existing levels of sales tax and import duties.

16 Preferential rate for British goods shown in right side of appropriate columns.

17 Preferential rates of GATT goods are shown in the right side of the appropriate columns. Additional duties charged are the municipal tax, wharf dues, stamp duty and expenditure tax (details on p. 88).

18 A number of countries specify a minimum absolute customs payment on imported bicycles – these include Nigeria, Rhodesia, Malawi, Kenya, Uganda, Tanzania and Pakistan.

19 Rate increases as cross-sectional width diminishes.

20 Except bicycle tyres and tubes (15 per cent).

21 Rate decreases with weight.

22 Cycle tubes, 20 per cent.

23 Suspended duty of 41 cents on certain tyres.

24 E$0·25 Kg for bicycles, free for trucks and lorries.

25 Bicycle tyres and tubes, 46 per cent.

exhaustive – it has been supplied by the Board of Trade, London, on the basis of information about taxes payable on exports to the countries concerned. The weight of these related duties varies considerably, being of far more importance in former French colonies, India and Turkey than the former British colonies (with the possible exception of Ghana).

(a) Ghana – purchase tax on vehicles (10 per cent–100 per cent).

(b) Pakistan – sales tax on duty paid value, defence surcharge on existing rates of sales and import duties.

(c) India – excise duties plus various surcharges on import duties.

(d) Ethiopia – transaction tax of 12 per cent on c.i.f. price plus 1 per cent; sales tax of 1 per cent on c.i.f. price plus 1 per cent.

(e) Turkey – municipal tax (15 per cent of customs duty), wharf dues ($2\frac{1}{2}$ per cent of c.i.f. invoice value plus customs duty plus municipal tax); stamp duty (5 per cent of value of goods), expenditure tax (15 per cent vehicles, 20 per cent bicycles).

(f) Tanzania – registration tax on private motor vehicles (between 10 per cent and 20 per cent of duty paid value depending upon engine size).

(g) Congo (Kinshasa) – tax of 3 per cent on the c.i.f. value of all goods.

(h) Algeria – production tax on all imports at duty paid price (private cars, tyres and tubes for private cars, 37–93 per cent; all other vehicles and parts, 20–45 per cent).

(i) Morocco – special tax ($2\frac{1}{2}$ per cent c.i.f. value) stamp duty (1 per cent value of customs duty and special tax), transaction tax (normally 8 per cent of c.i.f. value plus customs duty, special tax and stamp duty).

(j) Tunisia – production tax (varying between 14 per cent and $22\frac{1}{2}$ per cent of the duty paid value), consumption taxes (varying between $8\frac{1}{2}$ per cent and 36 per cent of the duty paid value), consumption duties (on tyres and private cars).

Many comments could be made on table 3·A1, but we content ourselves at this stage with one or two. The first is the sheer complexity of the system and the difficulty of comparing like with like. The second is the comparison between taxes on vehicle parts and on vehicles. In some countries, more or less the same rate of duty is imposed (e.g., East Africa) but in others it is less on parts. We shall return to this point later.

Appendix 3B

Motor Fuel Taxes and Prices 81

We intend to focus on three points: the relative duties imposed on gasoline and diesel fuel, the pattern of retail prices at ports relative to that of duties and the disparities between port and up-country retail prices.

In most countries gasoline duties are significantly higher than those on diesel fuel, the main exception being Nigeria and the three East African territories. We shall return to this point later in chapter 4.

Table 3·B2 shows the relations between duty rates and retail prices. Although the table has to be interpreted with some care (allowance being made for differences between port areas and inland cities, the effect of domestically available supplies on oil company pricing, and possible omissions and exemptions in the list of duties payable especially in Algeria, Morocco and Tunisia) it would seem that there is a fairly general tendency for local prices including duty to be correlated with duty rates. In view of the limitations of the data, there would not be much point in calculating a correlation coefficient – but the rough assumption that, by and large, local duties are passed on to consumers does not seem all that far out.

The enormous differences between gasoline prices in remote and accessible areas are shown in table 3·B3. Similar sorts of differentials apply to diesel fuel prices.

Table 3·B1 Duties on Gasoline and Diesel Fuel, March 1966

Country	Type of duty	Rate in pence per imperial gallon	
		Gasoline	Diesel fuel
Tunisia	Import	54·00	12·30
Algiers	Excise	52·68	32·18
Morocco	Excise	32·63	23·34
Sierra Leone	Import	26·40	19·80
Ghana	Import	39·00	17·00
	Excise	14·00	7·00
Nigeria	Excise	21·00	21·00
Congo	Import	2·25	0·66
(Kinshasa)	Consumption tax	12·51	—
	Statistics tax	0·10	0·10
Kenya	Import duty		
Tanzania	Consumption tax	22·20	22·20
Uganda	(Kenya)		
Zambia	Import	—	3·00
	Sales tax	6·00	—
Malawi	Import	—	6·00
	Sales tax	19·00	—
Ethiopia	Highway improvement tax	35·10	29·00
	Municipal tax	3·10	3·00
	(Both payable at port of entry		
	to Royal Ethiopian Customs)		
Cameroun	NA	27·74	14·53
Congo			
(Brazzaville)	NA	26·98	3·29
Gabon	NA	44·37	4·87
Central African			
Republic	NA	21·45	4·87
Chad	NA	13·48	17·43

Source: Shell International Petroleum Company, Ltd.

Note: On the basis of $2·8 = £ sterling, conversion of the data to US cents per US gallon would reduce each figure slightly (e.g., Tunisia gasoline figure is 52·5 US cents per US gallon).

APPENDIX 3B: MOTOR FUEL TAXES AND PRICES

Table 3·B2 Gasoline – Duties and Retail Prices, March 1966

Country	Duty payable (pence per imperial gallon)	Retail price (pence per imperial gallon)
Ethiopia (Addis Ababa)	40	64
Kenya (Nairobi)	22	54
Tanzania (Dar-es-Salaam)	22	50
Uganda (Kampala)	22	56
Algeria (Algiers)	53	71
Morocco	33	57
Tunisia	54	66
Malawi	19	49·5
Zambia (Lusaka)	6	44·5
Ghana (Accra)	53	72
Nigeria (Lagos)	21	44
Sierra Leone	26	53
Gambia	25	56·5
Gabon (Libreville)	44	84
Cameroun (Douala)	28	57

Sources: Shell International Petroleum Company Ltd and Board of Trade, London.

Note: 1. Prices at ports if not otherwise stated.
2. In principle all duties (and not just import duties) are included.
3. Local currency data converted into sterling at Brussels mean rate for May 1966.

Table 3·B3 Coastal and Non-coastal Gasoline Prices, March 1966

Country		Coastal town price (pence per imperial gallon)	Non-coastal town price (pence per imperial gallon)
Algeria	Algiers	71	—
	Tamanrasset	—	118
Nigeria	Lagos	44	—
	Kano	—	56·5
Congo	Kinshasa	38	—
	Bukaru	—	71

Sources: Shell International Petroleum Company Ltd. and Board of Trade, London.

Appendix 3C
African Railways — Financial Performance

The following points should be considered in the interpretation of the data:

(a) Railway administrations often have subsidiary interests in other forms of transport. In some instances separate accounts are shown for railway activities, whereas in other cases they are aggregated. The general policy has been to indicate the operating ratio in respect of railway activities alone if possible. In other cases the operating ratio relates to all the activities of the administration (even in these cases, the other activities are very minor and are not believed to have a substantial influence on the operating ratio)

(b) The operating ratio is defined as:

$$\frac{\text{working expenditure on railway activities}}{\text{gross receipts derived from railway activities}} \times 100$$

Working expenditure includes provision for depreciation as recorded in the accounts of the administration concerned. Unfortunately, there is little information about the bases on which these depreciation provisions are made and so there may well be an element of non-comparability of the data. In some cases *some* provision has been made in the working expenditure estimate for depreciation at higher rates than would be required on an historical cost basis – but, probably without exception, insufficient provision has been made on a replacement cost basis.

(c) In addition to the operating ratio, some attempt is made to indicate overall financial performance after allowance for miscellaneous interest receipts, general administrative charges not included in working expenditure and interest payments on capital borrowed. This financial performance relates to the undertaking as a whole, and not simply to railway activities. Furthermore, it is conditioned by the general level of interest charges on capital, which can vary considerably from undertaking to undertaking.

The overall conclusions seem to be that although some of the more important of these enterprises are still in a satisfactory position financially, the majority is now finding it difficult to cover costs. This picture would be even clearer if appropriate adjustments to conventional depreciation figures were to be made.

1. *Sierra Leone Railways*

	Per cent of railway working expenditure to railway receipts
1959–60	156
1960–1	142
1961–2	152
1963–4	131

Source: *Reports of the Railway Department* and *World Railways*.

In 1960–1 working expenditure was £1,056,000 and loan charges were £20,000. The deficit on recurrent account (before loan charges) was £308,000 (in 1959–60 it was £399,000). The government subsidy (including finance of non-recurrent expenditure) was £326,000 in 1959–60 and £185,000 in 1960–1. It is not possible to determine from the Reports whether depreciation was on a historical or replacement cost basis.

2. *Sudan Railways*

	Per cent of railway working expenditure to railway revenue
1957–8	73
1958–9	76
1959–60	70
1960–1	68
1961–2	67
1962–3	64
1963–4	61

Source: *Sudan Railways Annual Reports*.

Working expenses are calculated before provision for interest payments and additional depreciation provision for higher replacement costs. Interest is paid on fixed interest bearing stock at rates varying between 4 per cent and 5⅜ per cent.

3. *Ghana Railways*

	Per cent of working expenditure (including renewals) to total receipts
1958–9	101
1959–60	89
1960–1	82
1961–2	82
1962–3	88
1963–4	90

Source: *Administration Reports of Ghana Railways.*

In all years except the first, the balance on net revenue account was sufficient to meet interest payments. Of its £G20m borrowed capital, £G13m was borrowed from the government at 3 per cent and the remainder was supplied by the government, interest free.

4. *Trans-Zambesia Railway Company Ltd*

	Per cent of working expenditure (including renewals) to total receipts
1959	74
1960	75
1961	74
1962	78
1963	87
1964	82
1965	65
1966	53

Source: *Accounts* of the Company.

In recent years the Company has had an insufficient balance on revenue account to pay the £1·5m interest on debenture stocks (5 per cent) and a dividend on the 600,000 £1 ordinary shares.

5. *Malawi Railways Ltd*

	Per cent of working expenses (including provision for renewals) to gross receipts
1956	65
1957	66
1958	68
1959	74
1960	75
1961	76
1962	79
1963	84
1964	83
1965	82

Source: *Malawi Railways Annual Report, 1965*

Prior to the review of depreciation rates in 1965, depreciation provisions were substantially too low in relation to replacement costs.

6. *Rhodesia Railways Ltd*
Financial Results, 1960–6 (£000)

Year	Railway revenue receipts	Railway working expenditures	Rail Surplus transferred to net revenue account	Interest payments (all)	Contribution to sinking funds (all)	Surplus or deficit for year (all)	Operating ratio (per cent)
1960	31,357	25,089	6,268	3,629	920	1,446	80
1961	32,127	25,794	6,333	3,697	924	1,648	80
1962	30,921	27,481	3,440	3,672	993	−607	89
1963	32,175	28,508	3,667	3,649	1,226	−742	89
1964	34,868	27,766	7,101	3,653	1,337	2,267	80
1965	37,088	30,615	6,473	3,653	1,376	1,882	83
1966	39,408	34,984	4,423	3,630	1,368	4,190	88

Source: *Rhodesia Railways Annual Reports.*

The Sinking Fund provision is additional to the provision for depreciation, based on historical cost, which is included in working expenditure. Interest rates payable vary between $2\frac{1}{2}$ per cent and $6\frac{3}{4}$ per cent.

D*

7. *Benguela Railway Company*

	Per cent of working expenses to railway receipts
1955	60
1956	50
1957	55
1958	61
1959	61
1960	54
1961	60
1962	61
1963	64
1964	67
1965	68

Source: *Benguela Railway Company Annual Reports.*

Despite fairly heavy administrative charges on net revenue account the Company has been able to maintain a dividend of 10 per cent on ordinary share capital. Moreover, it should be noted that the railway is a concessionary company and that all assets of the company revert to the Portuguese government at the termination of the concession later in the present century.

8. *South African Railways and Harbours*

	Railway total working expenditure as per cent of railway total earnings
1958–9	74
1959–60	67
1960–1	65
1961–2	81
1962–3	83
1963–4	80
1964–5	83
1965–6	88

Source: *Annual Reports of South African Railways and Harbours.*

In all of the above years, except 1959 (when exceptional expenditure items were charged to net revenue account), there was a surplus after all interest payments (4 per cent–5 per cent) had been made.

9. *Nigerian Railway Corporation*

	a. Operating expenses as per cent of operating revenue
1955–6	81
1956–7	85
1957–8	94
1958–9	86
1959–60	103
1960–1	107
1961–2	96
1962–3	93
1963–4	89
1964–5	110
1965–6	113

Source: *Nigerian Railway Corporation Annual Reports.*

	b. Net income before tax (after payment of interest) (£,000)
1955–6	1,047
1956–7	1,404
1957–8	98
1958–9	1,097
1959–60	−1,350
1960–1	−2,335
1961–2	−1,064
1962–3	−940
1963–4	34
1964–5	−3,441
1965–6	−4,207

Source: *Nigerian Railway Corporation Annual Reports.*

10. *Ethiopian Railways*

a. Franco-Ethiopian Railway (E$,000)

Year	**1** Total receipts	**2** Operating expenses (excluding provi- sion for renewals)	Operating ratio $\frac{(2)}{(1)} \times 100$	Total expenses (including renewal expenses and financial charges)
1958	10,982	9,039	82	10,950
1959	11,563	8,954	77	10,998
1960	11,793	8,732	74	11,793
1960–1	12,015	9,073	76	12,075
1961–2	13,906	10,107	73	13,922
1962–3	14,156	10,798	76	14,106
1963–4	15,429	11,857	77	NA
1964–5	14,674	11,428	77	NA

Source: *Ethiopia Statistical Abstract, 1964,* and *World Railways.*

b. Agordat-Massawa Railway (E$,000)

Year	Total revenue	Operating expenses	Operating ratio
1956	2,262	2,208	100
1957	1,977	1,997	100
1958	2,000	1,927	97
1959	1,938	1,900	100
1960	1,991	1,653	83
1961	2,250	2,073	90
1962	2,499	1,931	77

Source: *Ethiopia Statistical Abstract, 1964.*

Note: No details are available on the coverage of operating expenses nor are data available on overall financial performance.

11. *East African Railways and Harbours* (£m)

Year	Total railway earnings	Railway working expenses (including renewal contribut- tions)	Gross surplus	Loan charges	Balance transferred to appro- priation account	Operating ratio
1958	18·9	15·9	3·0	3·0	Nil	84
1959	19·5	15·9	3·6	2·9	0·7	82
1960	19·7	16·5	3·2	2·9	0·3	83
1961	19·6	16·6	3·0	3·2	−0·2	83
1962	20·1	17·3	2·8	3·4	−0·6	86
1963	21·0	17·6	3·4	3·7	−0·3	84
1964	21·6	18·3	3·3	4·0	−0·7	85
1965	23·0	18·8	4·2	4·4	−0·2	82

Source: *East African Railways and Harbours Administration Annual Reports.*
Note: Data exclude harbours.

Notes

1 Government of India, Planning Commission, *Final Report, Committee on Transport Policy and Coordination*, New Delhi, January 1966, p. 11.

2 *Ibid.*, chapter 12.

3 Stanford Research Institute, *The Economic Coordination of Transport in Nigeria*, Stanford, February 1961, p. 88. Columbite is an example of a raw material export *not* favoured by the tariff – perhaps because it is largely mined by non-Nigerian companies.

4 Stanford Research Institute, *op. cit.*; E.K.Hawkins, *Road Transport in Nigeria*, HMSO, London, 1958.

5 In Nigeria, £1=20/- and 1/-=12d. The £N was at par with sterling until the devaluation of the latter in November 1967.

6 *Elias Commission of Enquiry*, Federal Government Printer, Lagos, 1960. The Memorandum submitted by Nigerian Railway Corporation (p. 67) argued that average cost per passenger mile fell from 2·06d for a 50-mile journey to 0·57d for a 700-mile journey.

7 The Stanford Research Institute inquiry, *op. cit.*, cited upper and lower limits for bus and lorry fares in the various Regions; the lowest was 0·6d per passenger mile in the West, which brings out that the railway had some advantage for really long journeys.

8 Federal Government, *Sessional Paper No. 1*, 1965.

9 *Ibid.*

10 Cf. Gilbert Walker, *Traffic and Transport in Nigeria*, HMSO, London, 1959, p. 161, for an illustration of this point in respect of cocoa charging rates as far back as 1931.

11 There is one system for the three countries: Kenya, Uganda and Tanzania.

12 It might be noted that this injunction has existed side by side with differential taxes on exports in Uganda for many years, i.e., with one arm official policy has helped farmers whereas it has hindered them with the other.

13 100 cents=1 shilling; 20 shillings=£1EA.

14 Cf. A.Hazlewood, *Rail and Road in East Africa*, Blackwell, Oxford, 1964, for details of studies.

15 *East Africa Sessional Paper No.1*, 1964.

16 A.Prasad, *Indian Railways*, Asia Publishing House, London, 1960, p. 242.

17 Cf. *Committee on Transport Policy*, p. 56, e.g., the ratio between the rates for the highest and lowest wagon loads for a 1,000-km journey was reduced from 5·3 in March 1964 to 2·93 in April 1965.

18 *Committee on Transport Policy*, p. 319.

19 *Ibid.*, appendix 7.

20 *Report of Road Transport Reorganisation Committee*, Delhi, 1959, pp. 21 ff.

21 *Committee on Transport Policy*, p. 316.

22 See appendix 3C for general statistics about railway operations in a wide range of African countries.

23 Elias Commission, *op. cit.*

24 *Ibid.* One complaint was that a Permanent Way Inspector extracted 99 bottles of beer out of his subordinates in return for promotion promises! See also *Tribunal of Enquiry into Nigerian Railway Corporation, July–August 1966*, Federal Ministry of Information, Lagos, 1966, vols 1–6.

25 J.Johnson, *The Economics of Indian Rail Transport*, Allied Publishers, Bombay, 1963, put losses due to passengers travelling without tickets at 80 million rupees per annum, i.e., something like 5 per cent of total earnings from passengers.

26 Cf. Nicholas Kaldor, 'The Choice of Taxes in Developing Countries', in E.F.Jackson (ed.), *Economic Development in Africa*, Blackwell, Oxford, 1965, p. 163.

27 The 1966–7 estimate was £19m.

28 *The Economic Development of Uganda*, Johns Hopkins Press, Baltimore, 1962.

29 Strictly, the Kenya import duty on motor fuels is less than in other countries, but is effectively brought to the same level by a special consumption tax. In the 1966 budget, it was announced that import duty was to rise by 10 cents per gallon and that the special consumption tax was also to rise by another 10 cents, making the new rate 2·05 shillings per gallon instead of 1·85 shillings.

30 In 1964 a special charge was introduced on transactions in secondhand cars; the motive was to catch sales of cars registered in one of the other two territories.

31 Adjusting EACSO data, which are on a calendar year basis to fit the Uganda financial year (commencing 1 July) by attributing half the proceeds for one calendar year to the financial year ending in the middle of that year and half to the next.

32 See *Committee on Transport Policy*, pp. 114ff., for full details. To give one example only, yearly taxes on forty-seat buses vary from a minimum of 161 rupees per annum to 10,800 rupees per annum.

33 See, for instance, *Report of Local Finance Enquiry Committee*, Delhi, 1951; and *Report of Road Transport Reorganisation Committee*, Delhi, 1959. The latter report (p. 25) estimated that in 1952–3 the extra running costs of vehicles alone amounted to more than half the revenue from octroi and similar duties.

34 The Civil War which started in 1967 will obviously have further repercussions.

35 Since the above was written, more recent information shows that the gross receipts increased by some £3m in 1966, but increases in working expenditure and renewals contributions were such as to leave the net balance much the same as in 1965.

36 *Committee on Transport Policy*, p. 53.

37 See IBRD, *The Economic Development of Uganda*, for general discussion and A.R.Prest, 'Some Aspects of Road Finance in the UK', *The Manchester School*, September 1963, for application of the same principles to the UK. Further discussion is also to be found in *Road Track Costs*.

38 *Op. cit.*, pp. 173–4.

39 With revenue at £8·2m, expenditure was put at £21m on the current investment basis and £12·3m on the capital stock basis (including a rough figure of £1·7m for police expenditure, etc. as well as £4·1m for maintenance costs in both cases).

40 A.Adedeji, *A Survey of Highway Development in the Western Region of Nigeria*, Western Region of Nigeria, Ibadan, 1960.

41 From *Reports of Accountant General*. An estimate had to be made of the customs duties on vehicles, as these are not separated in the official accounts.

42 *Uganda Statistical Abstract*, 1965, and information supplied by Statistical Department, EASCO. Some elements of duty are omitted, see table 3·2 above.

43 *Op. cit.*, chapter 11.

44 These figures under-estimate the total a bit. Cf. table 3·1 above.

45 The difference between user charges and total expenditure is *not* the same as the cash surplus in respect of public transport operations as the latter includes loans and aid from abroad for these purposes; this was in fact substantial in Ethiopia (and other countries too).

46 *Basic Road Statistics of India* (Thirteenth Supplement).

47 The actual figure given is 529 million rupees but it is expressly stated that this is an over-estimate. See also W. Owen *Distance and Development*, Brookings Institution, Washington, D.C., 1968, p. 132 for an estimate for 1963–4.

48 *Op. cit.*

49 I.e., the former British, as opposed to Princely, states.

50 A.Carlin, 'Indian Transportation: A Sectoral Approach to Development Constraints', *Journal of Development Studies*, July 1967, p. 428, argues that total road taxes have been well in excess of the relevant costs in the 1960s.

51 Data from *Statistical Bulletin of Road Transport Undertakings in India*, 1960–1.

52 See *Committee on Transport Policy and Coordination*, chapter 6, for full details.

53 Cf. *Report of Motor Vehicle Taxation Enquiry Committee*.

54 United Africa Co., *Statistical and Economic Review*, September 1954.

55 Cf. Walker, *op. cit.*, chapter 6, for a full account.

56 For further details in respect of Kenya, see *Interim* (1959) and *Final* (1961) *Reports of the Committee Appointed to Examine the Transport Licencing Ordinance* (the Madan Committee), Nairobi, Kenya: and in respect of Uganda, *Report of the Road Transport Industry Committee* (Olwoch Report), Kampala, Uganda, 1963.

57 Cf. Stephen A.Marglin, *Public Investment Criteria*, Allen and Unwin, London, 1967, for extended discussion.

58 Carlin, *op. cit.*, p. 423.

59 See p. 54.

60 See e.g., Carlin, *op. cit.*; Hazlewood, *op. cit.*

61 For a most valuable survey of public enterprise operations in a large number of countries see Andrew H. Gant II and Guiseppe Dutto, 'Financial Performance of Government Owned Corpora-

tions in Less Developed Countries', *I.M.F. Staff Papers*, March 1968.

62 *Op. cit.*, p. 326. It should be noted that the revenue figures quoted do not include the total yield of import duties on automobiles, etc., but only that deemed to be in excess of a 'normal' yield.

63 Cf. Carlin, *op. cit.*, p. 415, in respect of Indian Railways.

64 See, for instance, the account of the reactions of water supply officials in the Caribbean to pricing principles in A.R.Prest, *Public Finance in Underdeveloped Countries*, Weidenfeld and Nicolson, London, 1962, p. 77.

65 p. 27.

66 pp. 33–4.

67 Carlin, *op. cit.*, p. 434.

68 *Report of Committee on Transport Policy*, Memorandum by M.R.Bonavia, p. 320.

69 Cf. Professor Bauer's well-known illustration in respect of West African retail trade, of sugar being sold by the lump and cigarettes individually.

70 For details of load factors of goods vehicles in India, see *Final Report, Committee on Transport Policy*, appendix 3.

71 This seems to be particularly important in Sierra Leone (cf. Transportation Consultants Inc., *Transportation Survey of Sierra Leone* (1963), p. 31), but not nearly so important with East African Railways (cf. *The Economic Development of Uganda*, p. 307).

72 Cf. Hazlewood, *op. cit.*

73 Hawkins, *op. cit.*, p. 90.

74 *Committee on Transport Policy, Final Report*, appendix 7.

75 Cf. A.M.O'Connor, *Railways and Development in Uganda*, Oxford University Press, Oxford, 1965, p. 161, for this point in relation to Uganda.

76 Louis Lefeber and M.Datta Chauduri, 'Transportation Policy in India', in Paul N.Rosenstein (ed.), *Pricing and Fiscal Policies*, Allen and Unwin, London, 1964, p. 100.

77 *Ibid.*, p. 98.

78 *Op. cit.*, p. 425. It should be added, however, that there has been some controversy about the relation of coal freight rates to costs. *Ibid.*, p. 424.

79 Cf. Hawkins, *op. cit.*, p. 103, and E.E.Pollock, *Journal of Transport Economics and Policy*, vol. 1, no. 2 (May 1967), pp. 232–4.

80 Cf. Carlin, *op. cit.*, p. 428, for further discussion.

81 We have to thank Shell International Petroleum Company Ltd. for invaluable help in preparing this appendix.

4 Possible Lines of Policy

Introduction

There are two broad ways in which one could formulate policy proposals. One could start from the theory end and set out an ideal system of road and rail charges which could be applied to developing countries; or, alternatively, one can start from the actual systems which prevail today and suggest improvements which might get one rather nearer to that desirable on theoretical grounds. It seems to us more sensible to adopt the latter approach. One reason is that we are not starting with a clean slate. We are not putting forward proposals for a virgin area without any previous legislation. On the contrary, one has to accept that one is dealing with systems of road and rail charges, often of complex character, which have been in existence for many years. So it seems much more realistic to start from these systems as they are. A second point is that one is more likely to keep one's feet on the ground in deciding what is feasible and possible within the foreseeable future if one tackles the problem from this end.

At the same time we must have some general theoretical desiderata in mind when formulating proposals. It seems to us that the two most important general aims are to procure a better alignment of costs and prices between different transport modes,

107

different commodities, different distances, etc., and to minimise overall public transport deficits. We shall shortly show in more detail how we interpret these ideas, but the general reasoning is that the better alignment of costs and prices is needed to minimise resource wastage and that the minimisation of deficits is required in the parlous budgetary conditions of most developing countries. As demonstrated in chapter 2, these two aims will be in conflict when we have a situation of decreasing costs. And even though there are cases where it is appropriate for public transport authorities to operate with a surplus rather than a deficit, it may well be that in practice the latter type of situation outweighs the former in importance. So on balance the conflict will still be there, but we shall try to show as we go along how we should propose to reduce it further.

The implication of the preceding paragraph is that we are cautious about arguments such as those that deficits should be incurred in transport because it is a *sine qua non* for growth, or that there should be overwhelming attention to particular pricing policies designed to favour particular sections of the population, whether distinguished by income, occupation or region of location. This is not to say that we rule out such considerations entirely. Rather, the line taken here is that these are only admitted exceptionally: that we accept them when there are very compelling reasons to do so rather than that they are actively pursued as goals of policy on their own. So both growth and distributional arguments will be viewed as special situations arising out of any modification of present transport charges and prices rather than as an integrated whole.

In the growth case, the view taken is that set out in chapter 2: that macro-economic considerations do not give any support to the idea that deficits should be incurred in public transport operations; rather, the argument is likely to go the other way. And insofar as particular charging arrangements for particular types of transport operations are likely to be especially beneficial, we shall essentially take care of this in our general discussion of price/cost alignment.

On the income distribution side, one can put forward an endless series of objectives which could potentially be reached by suitable pricing policies for services supplied or for factors hired. But, first of all, there is often a great deal of uncertainty about the overall results – partly that the repercussions of particular concessions (especially when the services provided are intermediate in character, as is often the case in transport) may be extremely complex and partly that individual concessions may tend to offset one another. It is extremely difficult to nail down these ramifications in countries with a great deal of statistical information, let alone those we are dealing with here. Then one must remember the usual result that transport pricing which favours particular groups or regions on distributional grounds may well have unwanted allocation effects, though the same point holds, of course, for many other types of taxation, subsidies, cash transfers, etc. All in all, it can be plausibly argued that the possibilities of reducing allocation efficiency and the rate of growth of output are so clear that governments in developing countries should eschew redistributional aims in their budgetary and financial policies. So we shall simply leave it that we regard distributional objectives as a secondary aim only, while at the same time being prepared to indicate as we go along those sorts of mechanisms which can potentially serve such objectives best.

Administrative Framework

Before coming to grips with the most appropriate means of financing public transport provision, it is necessary to sketch in the sort of administrative background we have in mind. We use the words 'sketch in' deliberately. For one thing, this is very much a matter which must vary in detail from one country to another; for another, it clearly involves expertise in disciplines other than economics. So it is emphasised most strongly that the purpose of this discussion is only to set out a general reference framework.

The first topic is the nature and constitution of any public organisation of transport. It is most important here to insist on the principle of one government department only. The existence of separate ministries for railways and for transport in India has clearly been a source of friction and of weakness in framing transport policies.[1] If this point is taken, the next is whether the operational arm of the department should be a straightforward sub-department of government or whether it should be some form of independent or semi-independent public authority.

There are various general observations to make on this question: for instance, the need to retain some control by the legislature over public bodies versus the well-known dangers of civil servants trying (and failing) to run a department on commercial principles. There is clearly no universal answer. Many countries have experimented with many forms of organisation and there is no doubt a great deal more still to be learned in these matters.

But whatever the precise constitutional form of the railway and roads organisation, its relations with other elements of government, especially the Ministry of Finance, have to be spelled out. One important question is the interrelationship between the accounts of such commercial or semi-commercial organisations and those of the central government. As this raises important and involved questions relating to earmarking of funds and the like, we shall look at this separately.[2] Another question is whether public agencies of this sort should be given financial policy targets, such as the requirement to earn a certain specified rate of return on their assets. As this is closely related to pricing policies, we shall leave this over too for the moment.[3] Another point is that, whatever the degree of independence about day-to-day operations, one would expect a Ministry of Finance in any country today to keep a close watch on capital expenditure plans of all public agencies, as well as of other arms of government. This is clearly essential for many reasons of economic policy. Once again the precise form and extent of control is not something we can discuss here, but we simply note that any public transport authority must expect to operate under this constraint.

There is also another front on which one must expect public scrutiny. It is no good imagining that any public authority can have complete freedom to adjust its prices without some sort of public investigation. Organisations of this sort frequently have some degree of monopoly power, and if they did not face the need to justify their actions at the bar of public opinion it would be only too easy to respond to, say, an increase in wage rates by raising prices rather than by looking for possible economies in operation. The *folies de grandeur* of which all public spending agencies in all countries are capable also need to be scrutinised regularly by some body which has both power and prestige. Therefore, we shall assume throughout that there is some form of public watch-dog with the job of keeping public commercial enterprises on their toes. We shall not have anything to say on the precise form this regulatory body should take, though it is important to remember that it should not be so powerful as to smother legitimate price increases. If price increases are pre-vented for political reasons, etc., and public organisations come to be dependent on subsidies, there are obvious dangers of inefficiency, quite apart from the overall budgetary conse-quences. So regulatory bodies have to walk a very narrow path between disallowing and allowing price changes.

So much for the relations between a public transport authority and the inner core of government. What about those between the authority and private sector transport interests? The main questions arising here are the nationalisation, partial or com-plete, of private road goods and passenger transport; and the control of private operations by licencing. Neither of these falls squarely within the scope of this volume and we shall not argue their pros and cons. But, to clarify the background against which we discuss charging problems and the like, we shall assume dogmatically that private sector road operations, both pas-senger and freight, continue to be important and that the strength of the arguments against regulatory licencing will be

111

more fully recognised in the future. Appendix 4A brings together some of the main arguments on the latter.

Direct Charges

We shall first of all have something to say about the appropriate definitions of costs. We shall then discuss the various sorts of road transport charges and subsequently rail charges. We finish with two further topics, one being the very important question of differentiation between urban and rural road users and the other being the administrative device of fixing target rates of return for public enterprise operations.

Cost definitions

If we are to have the general targets of cost/price alignment and deficit minimisation in mind, we must have some clear-cut definitions of costs. We have referred to some of the relevant points before[4] but it is important to bring them all together.

The various components can be listed as follows:

1. Current operating costs, e.g., escapable costs of running trains and buses, maintaining and policing roads, etc.

2. Capital charges. In principle, we want the replacement cost basis for renewable assets, and the alternative use value for non-renewable assets. We then need to estimate annual costs by 'suitable' interest and depreciation charges. We shall revert to this in a moment.

3. In principle, transport facilities, road and rail, should bear taxes to finance part of the costs of public overhead expenditures in much the same way as any other consumption good or intermediate good. It can be argued that if government departments make use of public transport facilities without any payment (e.g., no licence fees for army vehicles), this is an offsetting item; but the counter-proposition is that it would be preferable to make two entries in the books rather than none. Obviously, it is impossible to give any universal ruling on the kinds of addition to

112

be made. It must be a matter of calculation – perhaps very roughly – in each specific case, on the lines set out in chapter 2.[5]

4. Given the imperfections of capital markets in developing countries, it is wise to make an allowance to meet some of the capital costs of any major expansion of the transport network. Once again, one cannot be precise about the mark-up involved; it will very much depend on the rate of growth of the transport system, the ability to keep reasonable control over capital costs, the monetary and inflationary implications of additions to government or public enterprise borrowing, etc. In general, however, one would expect this to be more important in the case of roads than railways, especially in the light of our background assumptions about transport licencing.

Such are the basic components. The next question is how they have to be modified to take account of social/private cost divergencies. Leaving aside road congestion costs, there are two major elements which (fortunately) work in opposite directions.[6] First, there is the proposition that labour costs are administratively determined – whether as a result of union pressure or legal requirements or both – at levels above those of opportunity costs. Insofar as employers generally (and *a fortiori* public enterprises) find that they have to take on more labour than they need – or at the very least are prevented from dismissing labour they do not need – for distributional or political reasons, the total labour costs of running a railway or maintaining a road may be still further overstated. On the other hand, it is frequently argued that interest rates used in public enterprise accounts in developing countries – often of the order of 6 per cent or so – are too low, once one makes allowance for the opportunity costs of diverting capital from private to public enterprise, risk and uncertainty, and so on. Once again, we have to grapple with something which is likely to differ very considerably from one country to another, but the following examples may be relevant:

1. One pair of authors[7] came to the conclusion that the minimum acceptable yield on railway investment in India was 20 per cent net of depreciation.

113

2. The effective rate of interest on loans lent to commercial vehicle operators in India in the 1950s was 18 per cent.[8]

3. A survey of 1,333 joint stock companies in India came to the conclusion that the return on capital was of the order of 13–14 per cent (based on the rate of net income to net fixed assets and inventories at book values), but with some allowance for over-depreciation and under-statement of income.[9]

4. In Turkey in December 1965 'savings bonds' (i.e., government ten-year bonds compulsorily imposed on all income recipiants at a rate equivalent to 3 per cent of their income) were being sold at a price equal to one-third of their face value. As the bonds carried a rate of interest of 6 per cent tax free, this implies that private time preference must, under the conditions then ruling, have been of the order of 18 per cent, tax free, even if one ignores any capital gains which would arise if repayment were ever made in cash, as distinct from another bond issue.

A few swallows of this sort do not even begin to make a summer, but if one has to guess – and someone has to – the conclusion must be that interest charges are likely to be understated in normal public enterprise accounting practice, even when separate allowance is made, as above, for the contribution towards capital costs of major expansion. This point of itself would not be of great substance if one could show that the usual assumptions in such enterprises about lengths of life of capital equipment were too pessimistic, leading to unnecessarily fast write-offs. We know of no evidence to support this, however, and so the general conclusion about interest rates is likely to stand. On the other hand, we must remember that there are offsetting factors in the over-estimation of labour costs. So the overall addition to cover these social aspects is likely to be positive but small.[10]

So far we have only talked about the constituent items of total costs, but for better cost/price alignment purposes, we need to have estimates of marginal costs.[11] It will be clear enough already that one cannot aim at a refined adjustment of price to marginal cost for each tiny segment of public transport operations. One simply cannot close one's eyes to, for instance, the discontinuities and elements of jointness in railway costs. Even a large organisation like London Transport, with a great deal of technical expertise at its command, claims that it is necessary to do a good deal of averaging between on- and off-peak services, surface and underground transport, and inner and outer London, etc. It may be that a little less averaging would not come amiss in that particular case, but nevertheless the moral is there for rail organisations with far less in the way of costing information and of technical personnel to utilise it. Similarly, the general principle for allocating road costs to different classes of traffic is to look at the incremental costs of providing the necessary facilities – a winding track through the forest may be sufficient for cattle movement but a hard surface, as tough and straight as possible, may be needed for large trucks. Once again, we find that very firm conclusions on such an allocation are not yet available in a country like the UK, despite its relative wealth of statistical material.[12]

It must therefore follow that in many cases one cannot hope for much more than pricing on the basis of covering some concept of average costs – both in the sense of average rather than marginal and in that of an average over a number of routes and operations. This obviously falls far short of the ideal but one simply has to be realistic in such matters. At the same time, one should strongly endorse the idea of moving further towards long-run marginal costing[13] principles as the necessary statistical information and technical expertise permit.

Road charges
Although one cannot hope to have a close correspondence between charges imposed on different kinds of vehicles and the incremental road provision and maintenance costs occasioned by them, in practice a fair approximation is likely to be met by charging on a basis which takes both weight and distance travelled per vehicle into account. On this basis, one usually argues for a combination of taxes on motor fuel (primarily reflecting distance) and vehicle licence charges (reflecting weight).

Many variants of these individual components are possible and *a fortiori*, many variants of the combinations. Let us deal with vehicle licence charges first.

Licence charges. The first point in favour of these is that the marginal costs of collection are low, in that licences will have to be issued in some form anyway. So if there are alleged bad effects of this tax relatively to alternative methods of raising revenue, the relative cheapness of collection is a factor which must be weighed in the balance. One of the most important criticisms voiced against the usual pattern of licence charges seems to be that of too low charges on large vehicles. We have already seen that the maximum annual charge in Nigeria is £117; and a study on Sierra Leone[14] made the point that the maximum charge was reached at 3,700 lbs tare weight for a vehicle and that on grounds of road damage the graduation should go well beyond that. In fact, unduly low charging of heavy vehicles may be an example of the application of European idea without thinking of the implications[15]: the point is that the excess of the charges for heavy vehicles over mean-weight vehicles – the latter being much less in developing countries when *all* usage is taken into account – should be greater than in Europe on the grounds that incremental costs imposed are also likely to be greater. It may also be the case that heavy vehicles are owned by wealthier rather than by poorer operators and so from an income distribution view-point there may be something to be said for this policy. In any event, whatever the precise differential, it is clearly more sensible to regulate heavy vehicles by the pricing mechanism than by the arbitrary kinds of arrangements which seem to have prevented the licencing of trailers and semi-trailers in India.[16]

However, one should not give the impression that the countries concerning us here have a monopoly of error. France, for instance, is another example of a country where there may be some under-charging of heavy vehicles.[17] There are also a large number of complex points, many not easily amenable to statistical analysis, in settling the appropriate charges in an equitable manner.[18]

It might, incidentally, be noted that the costs imposed by a heavy truck consist not only of the directly associated wear and tear of the road surface but also of the losses imposed indirectly on other vehicles[19] by making it necessary for them to go more slowly because of poor surfaces. In other words, there is the possibility of losses of time to human beings and less intensive utilisation of vehicles for reasons other than the standard congestion argument. It should be noted, however, that these arguments about costs occasioned by heavy vehicles are largely alternatives. If surfaces are kept in good order, one has the direct costs of repair. If they are not kept in good order, one has losses due to delays, but direct costs of repairs are avoided.

Another defect in vehicle licence charging practices is the kind of nonsense found in India where the disparate arrangements of different localities make for the enormous inconveniences and wastes of double trans-shipments, etc. However, we have already dwelt on this and need not say more. The historical equivalents to sweeping away such impediments to trade would be some of the famous nineteenth-century reforms such as Gladstone's efforts on UK customs duties or the benefits of the Zollverein to the embryo Germany.

One possible reform might be worth thinking about in more detail. A system of charging for vehicle licences which is jointly related to original cost price and to age[20] would have quite a lot to be said for it. One might by this means introduce a certain amount of progression into the system, e.g., a new vehicle costing £1,000 might pay a fee of $2\frac{1}{2}$ per cent in the first year, whereas one costing £2,000 might pay one of 5 per cent. The graduation with age could be linear or non-linear depending on how much one wanted to encourage use of older vehicles. One advantage of a system of this sort is that it would automatically levy a higher charge over the years on the owner who covers a great deal of mileage in that he is likely to buy a new vehicle more frequently than a man who only covers a small mileage each year. So, unlike vehicle licences generally, it is to some extent a tax on usage. A second point is that it can be arranged so as to give great encouragement to conservation and continuing use of old vehicles. In countries with exceptionally limited availability of capital this is a most important consideration. One should not lose sight of the fact that vehicle repairs require skills which are not always available; but human capital of this kind is likely to be acquired more quickly than physical capital. Thirdly, one can differentiate between trucks and cars in whatever way one wants – so as to encourage diesel rather than gas fuel vehicles, or to discourage large cars relatively to small ones, or to exact a sumptuary element of tax from cars (more especially new cars) but not from commercial vehicles. So there is plenty of scope in a scheme of this kind for both influencing demand for different types of vehicle and for contributing towards income redistribution policy.

To operate a system of this kind would require adoption of the UK type of licencing system rather than the United States one, i.e., one where the licence plates belong to the vehicle rather than to the driver. It also requires the UK system (or something like it) of having a vehicle log-book. This would record the cost price and date of original purchase and would have to be produced each year so that the sum payable for the licence that year could be calculated. It would be impracticable to take second-hand prices into account as a base; but in countries experiencing rapid inflation this would be an advantage (in that older cars would be treated more leniently than newer ones) if a major objective is to conserve capital as much as possible. One cannot pretend that a system of this sort would have no disadvantages. It might, for instance, result in more evasion; or be a means of increasing paternalistic or regulatory attitudes on the part of the government. But at least it seems worthwhile examining in detail.

One last point is that if there is a strict quota of licences to be issued for some class of vehicles, as when the number of freight vehicles on the roads is restricted for one reason or another, the

118

opportunity should be taken to auction licences rather than allow surpluses to accrue to the private sector of the economy.[21]

Fuel taxes. Appendix 3C showed that taxes on gasoline varied greatly in 1966 between countries, e.g., 21d per imperial gallon in Nigeria and 54d in Tunisia. There are many reasons for this: in some cases lower fuel taxes are counterbalanced (from a revenue view-point) by higher licence or duty charges on vehicles whereas in others road users have much heavier total imposts; and the latter result may in turn be accidental or simply the old principle of grabbing all the revenue one can from the meekest victims in sight.

It is probably more rewarding to look at intra – rather than inter – country variations. To begin with, fuel prices vary a great deal between ports of entry and the hinterlands, at least in African countries. Thus, for instance, whereas gasoline cost 44d per imperial gallon in Lagos in March 1966, it cost 57½d in Kano. This has serious implications for road charging policy both as between rural and urban areas and as between one region and another; we shall return to it later. Then we have the diesel/gasoline differentials to which we have referred previously. By and large, as appendix 3B showed, tax rates are lower for diesel fuel than gasoline in many African countries, though not in Nigeria and East Africa. There are a number of reasons for encouraging the use of diesel fuel, such as economies of operating costs, longer lives of diesel engines, longer periods between overhauls, and so on. These are fully set out in the International Bank *Report* on Uganda.[22] Further points which might be made are that such differentiation helps trucks relatively to cars and that it is also likely to help rural areas relatively to metropolitan ones. We shall come back later to the significance of this latter point.

Customs and Excise Duties, Sales Taxes, etc. It seems best to consider the whole range of such duties together. As appendix 3A showed, there is a large variety of duties of this sort in

E   119 operation – import duties, excise duties, sales taxes, transaction taxes, local taxes, wharf duties, stamp duties, etc. – but they have a good deal in common. This is not to imply that they are anything like perfect substitutes. Quite apart from the international trade aspect of choosing import duties rather than excise taxes – a most important topic but one which is outside our scope here – there are a number of other considerations. First, the particular circumstances of a country may favour the choice of one type of tax rather than another, e.g., retail sales taxes are much more difficult to collect when there are many small sellers and many small transactions, as is often the case in developing countries. Second, the economic effects of, say, excise taxes imposed at manufacturing level may differ from retail sales taxes, e.g., in their repercussions on the degree of competition in distribution.[23] However, we shall content ourselves with these words of warning, and not discuss further the relative merits of taxes imposed at different stages of the production and distribution process.

What does stand out is the unnecessary complexity of many of these arrangements. Whether major reliance on import duties is to be preferred to excise taxes in any particular country or not, there are really no grounds for the higgledy-piggledy arrangements prevailing in some countries (see, e.g., the details in respect of Turkey and Tunisia in appendix 3A). It is easy to see how this happens: a Finance Minister in desperate search for more revenue finds it easier to clap on a tax which is ostensibly different from the old one than to raise the rates on the old one. But it is also easy to see that no one can possibly know the overall effects on the allocation of resources, the distribution of income and so on if they have to hack through jungles of this kind. So the first plea must be for greater simplicity of indirect tax arrangements while recognising that this in turn implies greater honesty of purpose on the part of governments, a virtue which is not always conspicuous by its presence.

When one looks at the differences in tax rates, there are a number of issues to consider. It goes without saying that one has to consider these rates alongside licence charges and fuel taxes.

120

But let us take that as read.[24] The first consideration is the relative rates of import duty on whole vehicles, on parts for local assembly purposes, and on spare parts. We usually find that parts for local assembly purposes are taxed at lower rates than whole vehicles. How far this is desirable depends on the degree of protection thought necessary for local assembly, bearing in mind that the value added component in local assembly is already protected by virtue of import duties on whole vehicles. If we compare spare parts with whole vehicles we find (appendix 3A) that the former normally attract lower duty rates. Given the scarcity of capital equipment and the need to conserve what there is of it, this seems sensible. There is also the point noted in respect of Kenya[25] that high rates of duty on spare parts makes for theft of them, with all the losses due to any consequent immobilisation of vehicles. Whether there is any case for differentiating between spare parts and parts for assembly purposes depends on the balance of the considerations above.

Whether passenger or freight vehicles should be taxed more heavily depends on such points as the exact system of licence charging. It might be argued that another one is the relative importance of moving freight cheaply relatively to people, but where joint passenger and goods operations are common (as in West Africa) this point loses its force. Relative taxation of buses and cars raises a number of issues: whether the former is a less capital intensive means of transporting people, what the disincentive effects are of imposing high taxes on cars, what the distributional effects are, and so on. We suspect that none of these is easy to assess, especially when it is remembered that cars (for these purposes) include a lot of taxis as well as private automobiles.

Finally, differential taxes can be used against heavy vehicles as in the licencing case. In fact, the point goes a bit further. If some spares (e.g., tyres) are readily attributable to one class of vehicle rather than another, the differentiation can operate at this level as well as at that of whole vehicles.

Such are the sorts of ways in which excise taxes, etc. can

121

differentiate between different types of vehicles, spare parts, etc. But it must be understood that in many cases the major objectives may well be tied to protection of domestic industry, rather than to a closer alignment of charges with the incremental costs imposed on the road system.

It is convenient at this point to mention another subject which straddles the discussion of both vehicle licencing and customs and excise duties. In the case of advanced countries one can reasonably restrict oneself to motor vehicles, but where one has a vast array of other users from animals to bicycles to bullock carts, one has to look a little further. It is probably simplest to rely on import duties for bicycles, though as with motor vehicles the further import substitution goes the more will some form of excise taxation be needed. The whole range of bullock carts, rickshaws and so on is much more difficult. If one does decide to ignore them, it must be for reasons of administration rather than logic. The case has been forcibly made in India[26] that bullock carts do cause severe wear and tear on rural roads. One estimate was that there were forty million in the whole country and that it would be possible to collect something like 180 million rupees per annum in tax from them in the form of licence fees.[27] Whether this is so or not, one must remember that the exclusion of such users from the tax base in developing countries is (on a comparative basis) rather like saying that small cars and trucks should not be taxed at all in more developed countries. It is exactly parallel to the argument about applying western scale direct tax rates at the same relative, rather than the same absolute, position in developing countries.[28]

Congestion taxes. These must be judged a non-starter in developing countries at present. As we have seen,[29] there is a great deal to be said for a congestion tax in major metropolitan areas in advanced countries, whether viewed as a means of correcting for externalities or as one of rationing scarce road space or simply as one of reducing the need to subsidise public transport as a whole from tax revenues. Even though there are many cities in developing countries, especially capital cities, with crowded roads, one can scarcely envisage this sort of measure being put into effect at this stage. For one thing, the congestion is much less purely due to mechanically propelled vehicles – humans, animals, and non-mechanically propelled vehicles (e.g., bullock carts in India) all play their part. This immediately raises critical questions of income distribution if a tax is imposed. And as for administration, even western countries have so far shrunk from the effort involved in such a system, although the indications are that the UK is slowly edging towards it. So the day when TV cameras record car numbers in the streets of Delhi or Lagos is still some way off. The moral is rather that the experience of western countries in allowing cities to be organised in such a way that a good deal of commuting between home and work has developed should be taken to heart. Although such a development may seem innocuous at the stage when people cannot afford their own cars and have to walk, bicycle or rely on mass transit facilities, all experience shows that once commuting by car becomes a habit it is very difficult to hold in check (let alone reverse); with the consequences, familiar to all of us, of having to choose between peak-hour bottle-necks and large-scale investments to relieve them. It is important to prepare for major innovations of the congestion tax kind before powerful political pressures are built up against them. To this end one would certainly like to see parking charges in city centres levied on a much more thoroughgoing basis than has hitherto been the case, even though they are likely to be a less efficient device than congestion taxes.[30]

Tollroads. Although the principle of toll roads is a very old one and although it has been put into operation in a number of countries in recent years (e.g. Mexico and Japan), we have found little discussion or enthusiasm for it in the countries investigated. There has been a somewhat half-hearted endorsement of the principle in India[31] and a rather fuller discussion in Kenya. The *Kenya Development Plan 1964–70* discussed in some detail the project for a toll road from Nairobi to Mombasa and outlined a plan to obtain professional advice on the collection of tolls, concessions to petrol stations and hotels, etc. and to keep an open mind about financing other road projects in this way. The principle has also been endorsed in many other cases,[32] but there the matter has rested.

One obvious argument against tolls is that if one has a small densely populated area, there will have to be a large number of entry and exit points and this will make costs of collection prohibitive. This has always been the position adopted in the UK, for instance, where there are a number of examples of tolls for bridges and tunnels but none for the new motorway system. But it is clear that there are many developing countries where such conditions do not hold. There are cases where roads joining major centres of population generating a lot of traffic pass through intervening, sparsely populated areas, thus lending themselves to limited access; and, in general, one would expect the labour costs involved in toll collection to be less important than in western countries – though questions of staff corruption or dishonesty have to be remembered. One can see the arguments, both theoretical and practical, against introducing tolls on roads which have been free to all kinds of traffic from time immemorial. But circumstances change if wholly new roads are built or if there are major reconstructions. And if there is any hope of attracting private capital into road construction on the basis of a share in the toll proceeds, this is obviously of major importance. On balance, one cannot help feeling that insufficient attention has been given to these possibilities in some countries, and that the obstacles have been blown up to larger than life size.

Road freight rates and passenger charges
When, in addition to highway ownership, we have direct government operation of freight or passenger services, we then have to look not only at the costs of providing and maintaining the road surface, but also at those of providing and maintaining the vehicles. The same general principles as before must operate:

roughly try to get relative prices in line with costs and be extremely careful about incurring deficits. The latter point is more than ever important here. First, there are always strong political pressures at work in the case of municipal bus authorities or similar ventures to keep prices down, even though costs may be rising substantially. Second, if public transport authorities do run at a loss, this will make it difficult for private competitors, current or potential, to make profits. This may, therefore, mean that private capital is no longer attracted to this field, thereby making it necessary for public authorities to extend the scope of their operations, thus increasing still further the drain on general revenues.

It is convenient at this stage to refer to one other point. Although the issue of flat-rate fares in cities versus fares graduated according to distance has to be faced whether public or private operators run the transport system, it has a slightly more direct character in the former case and so can reasonably be dealt with now. London Transport has always maintained that graduated fares enabled them to catch a number of passengers who would otherwise have chosen to walk short distances. Against this, there is the obvious disadvantage of the labour costs of collection.[33] There are also other points such as the relative importance of short and long journeys, the amount of competition over short distances from taxis, and the danger that flat-rate fares may encourage too much long-distance commuting. Given the relative plentitude of labour in the countries which concern us, one might have thought that the London type of argument would prevail. On the other hand, the control of a graduated fare structure is complex and it may well be easier to adjust fares to meet general price rises if they are on a flat-rate basis.[34]

Public loans for transport purposes
Loans made by public authorities on a 'non-commercial' basis clearly have financial repercussions. We found two types of transactions which have been of importance. One is that of

low-interest loans to government employees to buy cars. This was a well-known feature of many British colonies, and Hawkins,[35] for instance, estimated that nearly one-third of the capital expenditure on private cars in Uganda in 1957 was financed in this way – a much higher proportion than that financed by hire purchase. However, the importance of this practice seems to have diminished in recent years and so it is not necessary to spend more time on it.

The second example is that of loans to private road transport undertakings. Helleiner[36] records that large sums were lent for this purpose in Nigeria in the 1950s and also shows that some of these ventures were disastrous.[37] Although loan policies of this sort are not likely to be of major importance relatively to total road charges and expenditures, they must clearly be kept under firm control if they are not to negate other aspects of policy.

Rail charges
The role of railways in the future will be dependent on changes in total demand for the various kinds of transport services and on competition from other media – roads for freight and to some extent passengers, pipelines for oil products, and air for passengers. Given our proposition that the restriction of road transport by licencing should be of a very limited character, the most likely role for railways in the future is one of shifting heavy or bulky commodities over long distances; there will also be a role for transporting commuters in large urban areas and, for a number of large and/or poor countries, some long-distance movement of passengers as well. These are the sorts of things on which, as we saw in chapter 3, railways are likely to have comparative cost advantages.

We shall confine ourselves entirely to discussions of railway rate-making. In principle, indirect taxes on railway inputs or outputs also enter into the overall financial picture, but the principles at stake are essentially the same as those relating to roads and so we shall not say anything more about them.

The major changes needed in freight tariffs will be to switch them over to a cost basis, so that the relative rates quoted for particular cargoes on particular routes will be more closely related to relative costs than heretofore. No one should underestimate the magnitude of this task. First, even accepting the fact that some averaging between commodities, routes and times of the year is inevitable, the ascertainment of cost variations is still a major task which cannot be accomplished in the course of a few months. Major changes in tariff structures have been known to take years to come into effect in western countries, despite their much more adequate supply of suitably trained technical personnel. Second, procedures for changes in rail freight rates have often involved lengthy public procedures; these produce delays and also bias the results – in that objections will always be made to increases but never to decreases. Third, there are likely to be powerful arguments for exceptions to cost rules. For instance, the East African rail tariff favours Uganda by particular definition of mileage on particular routes. It is highly unlikely that particular arrangements of this sort could be lightly abandoned, even though there may well be some doubt about the precise results of such arrangements and even though one can argue that in principle it is much better to make transfer payments directly to particular regions or ethnic groups, on the grounds that one can thereby meet any income distribution objective without distorting the pattern of spending in the process. Despite these difficulties, there can be little question that attempts to put rates on to a basis which more adequately reflects cost variations by distance and by commodities (especially in relation to low-value, bulky goods) would reap many benefits in the form of less need for rail capacity extension, less distortion of producer choice of raw materials, less mal-location of plants, and so on.[38]

As for passenger fares, it is often argued that passenger operations are subsidised by freight operations at present.[39] Once again, a common prescription is that fares should be rearranged on a costs basis so as to eliminate such cross-subsidisation; but one has to be careful about this. There are inherent limits to the variations one can make in passenger fares and there must inevitably be a good deal of averaging between different days of the week or different weeks of the year. Second, when the railway system is, as in India, a means of mass transportation for the poorer sections of the community, suggestions for major increases in fares are unlikely to be very acceptable politically, despite the obvious possible disadvantages of the present arrangements in encouraging excessive mobility.

But however much change one can engineer in the rates structures of railways, the likelihood is that many of them will face deficits – possibly deficits on operating account, certainly deficits in respect of total outgoings. This is partly due to the slow processes of changing fares, closing down redundant stations, etc.[40] It is partly due to the powerful political position held by railway administrations anxious to preserve as much as possible of existing empires. Another point is that railways often have the worst of both worlds in labour matters: unions are strong enough to keep pushing up wage rates and yet as public bodies railways may have to employ more labour than they really need. The very real need to have some form or other of common carrier for freight and of standby service[41] for passengers, especially in countries with road systems liable to become impassable in the wet season, is another contributory factor. Finally, some of the indirect devices, which, as we shall see later, are sometimes possible in the roads case (e.g., charges for the benefit of providing access) are not readily adaptable to railways. Thus, the process of contraction (or at most very slow expansion) of railway facilities is likely to mean financial deficits[42] or particular devices to avoid them. To take one example of the latter, Hazlewood argued in his study of East African Railways that after adjusting to a cost-based tariff, and allowing for subsidies in some cases, some special restrictions on road oil transport might still be needed to help out the railways.[43] The less one is willing to countenance the continuance or new imposition of road transport licencing restrictions, the more one is likely to have to face such deficits.

Rural versus urban charges

An issue common to both rail and road is the level of charges imposed on rural, relatively to urban, transport users. In the case of roads, the standard of service provided is usually lower in rural areas, in that asphalt roads are much less common. Consequently more wear and tear per mile is experienced, and rural roads are often unusable in the wet season. These effects are reflected in Nigerian Marketing Board calculations of operating costs per ton (asphalt roads 6·5d, gravel 6·0–7·5d, dry-weather roads 9·0–10·0d)[44]; and Hawkins[45] found similar differences in E. Africa. However, these are cost differences incurred by users; how appropriate they are depends on whether user charges correctly reflect relative costs of provision and maintenance per mile of road. It is also a well-known feature of developing countries that vehicle ownership tends to be largely concentrated in urban areas. It can, therefore, be argued that rural roads are not likely to be as intensively used as urban ones and, if so, cost of provision and maintenance per vehicle mile (as distinct from cost per mile) may be greater than that of urban roads. On the other hand, if congestion costs are an element of charging policy, they are much more relevant to urban than to rural areas. So from some angles there is a case for charging rural roads users relatively less, and from others relatively more than urban users. One cannot generalise about where the balance of the argument rests, but in reaching any decision there is a further factor to consider. Large-scale population emigration from rural to urban areas with consequential increases in unemployment, crime and so on has become a very serious issue in a number of countries in recent years.[46]

So it may well be that, even though one cannot be certain about the present balance between road costs and charges, there is a case for being generous in charges to rural transport users in the hope that this will discourage emigration from rural areas to cities. The same general argument also applies to rail charges.

Practical ways of implementing these ideas in the case of roads are not nearly as easy as in that of railways which can offer concessions on agricultural products, tapering rates, etc.[47] A congestion tax on urban traffic could easily be combined with general reductions in licence and gasoline charges, so as to benefit rural areas, but we have ruled the former out as a non-starter in the foreseeable future. Probably the most one can do on the charges side is to make sure that charges such as those on property for access value are only applied in towns; and perhaps to have some element of differentiation in motor fuel prices, e.g., by keeping rates of tax on diesel fuel lower than on gasoline and by having slightly[48] lower tax rates on gasoline in up-country areas than in major cities or ports. But, at the very least, the present pattern of fuel oil prices of much higher levels up-country (see appendix 3B) needs to be looked at from this angle.

However, one must not overdo this argument of favouring rural areas by the mechanism of transport pricing. First, the influence on emigration to cities may not be very great in practice. Second, it is preferable on grounds of principle to raise incomes of rural areas more directly rather than help them by a process which may lead to over-use of transport facilities. So our final conclusion must be that this is a game to play with some caution.

Target rates of return
One might ask about the relevance of target rates of return in controlling public enterprise operations. This is a favourite device in some countries, e.g., target rates of return on book capital have been set in recent years for various public enterprises in the UK on the basis of principles set forth in a now famous official document.[49] It was laid down that over five-yearly periods, revenues should be sufficient to cover all costs (including interest, depreciation at replacement cost and contributions towards capital expenditures and contingencies). In a number of cases this obligation was expressed as a target rate of return (e.g., electricity 12·4 per cent gross or 6·7 per cent net of historical depreciation; gas 10·2 per cent gross or 6·5 per cent net).

130

It may well be that it is useful to specify objectives in this way to act as a spur to managerial efficiency or employee morale. But it must be realised that if one specifies a pricing policy in detail (including such items as the contribution towards capital expenditure) and if investment decisions are made in accordance with a specified discount rate, target rates of return do not add anything to operating rules. They are simply another way of expressing the same principles of policy in that if the basis for pricing is given and the stock of capital determined, a rate of return on that capital is implicit. Still less do target requirements, even when fulfilled, guarantee that all costs will be covered. Dying enterprises can have targets ('deficit not to be larger than . . .') as well as new-born ones. We must therefore conclude that such devices are in general an alternative, rather than a supplement, to the principles set forward here.

Indirect Financing

It is frequently argued that taxes or charges imposed directly on users should be supplemented by other taxes or charges designed to catch indirect beneficiaries from public transport facilities. It is important to make the distinction from the outset between technological and pecuniary externalities.[50] Technological externalities arise when the provision of public transport facilities affects the physical outputs other producers can get from inputs or the satisfactions consumers of other products obtain from their intake. An example would be when a new main road draws traffic away from neighbouring streets thereby making them safer, quieter, etc. Pecuniary externalities, on the other hand, are occasioned by shifts in factor or goods prices and essentially represent transfers from one section of the population to another, rather than changes in output or output/input relations. In the technological externality case, charges on indirect beneficiaries can be thought of as a justifiable supplement to those on direct beneficiaries; but in the pecuniary case they are primarily a substitute and can only be thought of as a supplement if for one reason or another charges on direct beneficiaries are judged inadequate.

The type of charge, as well as the people charged, will tend to differ from that found earlier. Whereas we were then involved in questions of vehicle and fuel taxes, rail tariffs, and so on, we now have to consider taxes on increments in land values and similar devices.

There are many historical examples of raising revenue in this fashion. We single out the experience of Uruguay here, for even though it is not one of the countries studied in detail, this particular aspect of its transport arrangements is extremely interesting.[51] Ever since 1928 there has been a system of feeding specific revenues into a 'Permanent Fund for Developmental and Farm to Market Roads'. In recent years this has been partly a tax on gasoline, partly one on tyres, and, what concerns us most here, a tax on property benefiting from road developments. This tax (which provides about one-third of the total revenue) is levied according to the type of road and the distance of the land from it so that, e.g., land within 6 kilometres of the road pays a higher rate of tax than land 6–12 kms from the road and so on. Annual rates, in fact, vary from 0·125 per cent to 0·65 per cent of the appraised value of land depending on the two variables. It is reported that yield has been disappointingly low in recent years for a variety of reasons – partly low appraisal values for land and partly the complications which arise when a given piece of land is near to two or more road developments, the general principle being that there should not be any double taxation. Nevertheless, it is an exceedingly interesting example of what can be done in this field.

Our second example relates to irrigation, not roads, but illustrates the principles all the same. Ever since early legislation in Mysore in 1888 there have been attempts in India to recoup some of the benefits from irrigation in the form of betterment charges. These have usually been partly levied on the cultivator (say, according to the volume of water used) and partly on the landlord (usually on the basis of differential capital values of wet and dry land).[52] No one would claim that this system has worked flawlessly either at the assessment or collection stages, but it is another illustration of what can be tried.

If one is to charge for public transport services in this way, there are certain general principles to be followed. The first is that the particular group of individuals benefiting from transport provision and the extent of their benefits must be readily identifiable. It must be recognised that this is a tall order. To give an illustration, one must be able to appraise the particular increment in capital value (due to, say, a new highway) of a particular piece of land, i.e., isolating this particular reason for capital increments from all others. But even if this obstacle is surmounted, there is a second. For clearly the charge levied should in principle bear some discernible relation to the benefit obtained; otherwise, there could be gross inequity between, say, neighbouring landlords. This immediately means that only taxes which bear a discernible relation to specific benefits should be considered as supplemental or alternative means of finance in this context.[53] For example, capital values of land will not be as good a tax base as increments in capital values, in that the latter will be more closely related to transport improvements than the former. Thirdly, it is likely, though not automatic, that local, rather than central, organisation and control of such taxes is desirable. A better appraisal of benefits and a greater willingness to pay for them are likely to prevail in that case.

With these general principles in mind, let us now turn to some of the specific suggestions one meets in this field. First it is often argued that roads provide access to property[54] as well as a means of movement and that not to charge for such a service would amount to under-taxation of a wide class of beneficiaries. In general, this argument clearly has substance, but the real problem is to obtain a convincing measure of the benefits[55] derived and a form of tax which is closely related to them. Property taxes are often suggested, but the relationship between them – whether they are based on capital or rental value of property – and benefits

133

of the access type is very distant. Furthermore, urban property taxes are in a sorry state in many of our countries in that assessments after often inequitable and out of date, and collection arrangements leave much to be desired.[56] But it would be utopian to expect a great deal more from them at this stage.

Partly because property rights are often difficult to disentangle and partly for administrative reasons rural property taxation is even more primitive in character; and in any case, we have said that the access element of this might be remitted if we wanted to favour rural areas in our charging system.

A particular form of indirect financing which might be considered for urban areas is special taxation of business premises in central locations. The argument is on these lines: the growth of businesses in city centres means a greater need for mass commuting facilities. The direct way of financing these would be to charge the users and this would in turn react back on employers through claims for compensating wage increases. But if there are political or institutional obstacles to such a course, an alternative would be to levy a special tax on the firms concerned. Obviously this is an nth best solution. Given the state of property taxation in many cities, it would be extremely difficult to avoid harsh discrimination between firms if this were the basis of the extra tax. Perhaps a better way would be an employment or pay-roll tax, but the connection between numbers employed, or pay-rolls, and demands on mass transit facilities is far from uniform, quite apart from collection problems with small enterprises. But even an nth best solution is better than none at all, and so it may be a possible device to have in reserve.

There are two further points. One is that it is very common to give tax concessions to new enterprises in developing countries, usually in the form of special depreciation allowances or of relief from liability to taxation of profit for a period of years. Something might be done about the costs of new roads which have to be provided to service such factories, hotels, etc. One might, for instance, offer new enterprises an option: *either* the normal tax concessions together with the stipulation that they provide the

134

necessary road access links *or* if roads have to be publicly provided, the size of the tax concessions should be *pro tanto* reduced. It is extremely easy in making tax concessions to new enterprises to look only at the gross benefits they create, forgetting that there may be a number of costs imposed at other points in the economy. So any system which forces the authorities to consider such matters has much to be said for it.

The second is the use of local voluntary labour for road-building. If it can be demonstrated that the local benefits of such road-building are tangible, then this form of 'taxation' has a lot to be said for it, in that there is a discernible relation between the two. It has, of course, been used in many countries at many times, especially for rural road-building.[57] Equally clearly, it has its limitations: it may be difficult to provide any necessary finance from local resources, labour may not be available at the time of year best suited to road-building, one can get an earth road that way but an asphalt one is much more difficult, and exhortations to work for such purposes rapidly run into diminishing returns. So it would be inadvisable to rely too much on this mechanism.

We come now to taxes on increments in land values. There are a number of closely related issues here. One is that in discussing the benefits arising from new or improved roads one must not fall into the trap of counting the same thing twice over or of failing to net out decreases from increases in land values. It is normally argued,[58] for instance, that it would be double counting to include as a travel benefit the extra rents received by owners of garages, restaurants, etc. on a road which is improved, when time and cost savings to road users have already been estimated on a comprehensive basis. We can also argue that, if GNP increases as a result of, say, a new road connecting two hitherto isolated communities, this reflects *either* extra spending *or* extra factor rewards but not the sum of the two. At the same time, it may well be the case that direct user charges do not appropriate anything like all the benefits arising from an improvement or new development, and that there is a substantial

135

rise in land values. This may be particularly so when a new railways line or road opens up a hitherto remote area;[59] many would argue that in cases of this kind this is a clear-cut gain, even if in other cases (e.g., road improvement resulting in traffic diversion) there are decrements as well as increments in land values.[60]

This immediately brings us face to face with all the arguments about taxing capital gains. First, there is the general issue whether capital gains of any kind should be taxed; second, the further issue whether capital gains due to rises in land values should be taxed at a different rate to others.

Most writers on public finance would now argue that capital gains (net of capital losses) are a form of income and so should not be outside the income tax net altogether. On the other hand, there is still some disagreement on whether normal income tax rates or concessionary rates should apply to capital gains; and whether allowances should be made for changes in the general level of prices or changes in interest rates, so that only 'pure' capital gains are subject to tax. There is a vast literature on the subject which it would be impossible even to summarise here.[61] It is sufficient for our present purposes simply to accept the view that in principle there is a case for subjecting capital gains to taxation.

The second question is whether increments (or decrements) in land value should be taxed at a different rate to other capital gains. There is no obvious reason for saying that they should be taxed at a lower rate. Indeed, in developing countries where there is a high ratio of land value to reproducible physical capital, such a proposition would be akin to having Hamlet without the Prince. So where there is a general capital gains tax in operation we should clearly expect this to set the minimum level of rates for taxing land value changes. On the other hand, it can be argued that increments in land values should be taxed at higher rates than other capital gains and, in particular, that there is a case for taxing such increments even if there is no general capital gains tax at all. A further extension of this argument is to say

136

that increases in land values due to transport improvements should be fixed at higher rates than increases in land values due to other causes.

Surely one must be cautious here, especially on the latter point. Specific connections between transport developments and land gains are not always easy to establish. There are many other reasons for land gains; and the direction of causation may indeed be reversed so that the rise in land values precedes the transport improvement, e.g., an industrial development raises land values and also roads have to be built as a consequence. So a capital gains tax system which is confined to one particular type of gain due to one particular type of cause is likely to run into trouble. There may be a stronger case for taxing land gains in general at higher rates than other capital assets. Legislation to this end was passed in the UK in 1967, for instance.[62] But the administration of such a tax is likely to be closely bound up with the land use planning laws of a country and so it is not easy to generalise about it. The final reflection must be that in countries where the administration has found it difficult to cope with a general capital gains tax – and this after all is the position in most countries in the world, not just those we are covering here – the possibilities of isolating particular types of gains and taxing them at differ-ential rates are far from bright. And in those countries where it is extremely difficult to pin down land tenure and ownership and say how much of what belongs to whom – and this is the case in many parts of Africa – the difficulties are all the greater.

The Financing of Deficits

Justifiable reasons for deficits
Even after making the fullest use of the various devices for direct and indirect financing of public transport operations, it is likely that there will be a number of cases where financial help is needed. One example is that of the sparsely populated country with a low current level of economic activity. Although one

137

should not exaggerate the degree of indivisibility in transport capacity – one can do quite a lot with one-way operations and regular passing places on both road and rail – one can see that there are likely to be minimum structures technologically, especially with railways, which may still be too large for profitable operation at the current level of traffic. Where there are very strong arguments for helping out a particular part of a country for, say, distributional reasons, even though there is no long-term expectation of greater usage, or where deficits are general in a country but there is long-term expectation of greater usage, there is a respectable case for financial assistance. There are clearly examples of such situations in the less densely populated countries of Africa.

The second common case is that of the unintentional deficit[63] where there has been an unexpected fall in demand or increase in costs so that the system, or at least components of it, are working well below capacity. This applies pre-eminently to the railways in many countries. The element of subsidy needed will depend on a wide variety of factors, and not least the degree of restriction placed on entry into the road industry, but it should be viewed as a temporary measure to bridge the gap, while some process of contraction gets under way. The outpayment necessary will depend on the capital structure of the railway organisation. If there are any equity shareholders, one can envisage an effective reduction in size of financial liabilities to match the reduction in size of the real assets; but if there are only bondholders, or if the equity element is very small, the need for public support in writing down financial obligations will be that much greater. In fact, the latter is much more likely than the former.

A third case is the second-best sort of situation. Thus it might be argued that the optimum set of transport charges in urban areas would be where, on the one hand, privately owned vehicles pay a congestion charge, and investment in highways is in accord with tax receipts from this source,[64] and, on the other, that mass transit should be made to stand on its own feet without public subsidy. But if there are institutional or administrative reasons

138

why one cannot levy this sort of congestion charge (e.g., costs of collection), the next best policy may be to collect less revenue from private road users, to build fewer highways and to subsidise mass transit.[65] This is only a second-best policy in the sense that urban transport as a whole will tend to be under-priced relatively to other goods and services with consequential undesirable effects (too many resources drawn into it; over-encouragement of suburban living, etc.) but it may nevertheless be the most feasible policy to pursue.

Finally, there is the case where the public transport system is expanding rapidly but where it is difficult to raise sufficient additional funds on the capital markets, domestic or foreign, for institutional or other reasons.[66] Although this is not deficit finance, as in the other cases, it will nevertheless be a call on government funds.

Such are the major reasons why funds may still be needed even after following any or all of the suggestions about direct and indirect financing. We now have to explore two questions: one is the various ways in which financial assistance may be given and the second is the repercussions on government finances.

Forms of financial assistance
The form best taken by financial assistance is to some extent dependent on the reason for it. If it is judged that the interests of particular industries, regions or groups of individuals dictate a larger transport network than is 'commercially' viable, an appropriate solution would be to pay grants to these particular producers, regions, etc. and then let them pay the full cost of the transport service. Individuals will then have a better idea of the value of the concessions, particular ministries will have to shoulder the responsibility of looking after the interests of particular industries, and so on.[67]

In cases when financial assistance is given directly to a public enterprise, it can take a number of forms. It may, first of all, be in the form of an outright grant or in the form of a loan, with or

139

without interest payments. Loans assistance may in turn be direct or in the form of a government guarantee attached to the authority's own bond issue. There are some cases where loans with interest are appropriate, e.g., where there is an expectation of a temporary deficit with subsequent large surpluses or where the finance is needed for extensions of capacity. By and large, the case for loans without interest rather than outright subsidies is likely to rest on administrative convenience, effects on operating efficiency, and so on.[68]

If one settles on a subsidy, the remaining question is whether it should be a lump sum amount per annum or whether it should be geared to some particular type of revenue or expenditure. For instance, in France contributions are made to French Railways on the basis of one subsidy for permanent way expenses, another for pension funds and another as compensation for special losses.[69]

Although there are some cases where subsidies can readily be tied to particular actions or items of expenditure (e.g., they may be made conditional on scrapping plant and equipment when the purpose of the subsidy is to tide over an enterprise until it can contract in size) one must be careful – it is so tempting for management not to exert itself but rather to manipulate a deficit so that it all appears as part of the subsidised account irrespective of whether it 'really' belongs there or not. At the same time, if one fixes a sum in advance to meet special responsibilities (such as is proposed in the UK to help the railways keep open branch lines for social reasons),[70] one still has to obtain a measure of the financial cost of such special responsibilities – and a measure which does not rapidly get out of date.[71]

Repercussions on government finances
The last topic in this section is the repercussions of public enterprise subsidies etc., on the general finance of government. The question is whether the finance should be found by raising more taxes, reducing other expenditures, or borrowing. In some cases, as when there is an international loan or grant tied to a specific

transport project, the query may not arise – but let us leave that on one side, not because it is unimportant but because it is clear-cut. In cases where choices have to be made many questions arise, some of which can only be answered in the context of a particular country at a particular time, e.g., whether aggregate demand is insufficient or not. But, there are some particular points on which we must spend a little time. The first is the pro-position that if one element of public transport has to be sub-sidised, some other element in the transport sector must be taxed, e.g. it is sometimes argued that the net yield from road, etc. taxes should be sufficient to cover rail deficits or that mass transit should be subsidised by taxes levied on private vehicle users. Unless one holds the view that public transport should be run as a self-balancing, earmarked set of accounts – and we shall come to this shortly – this seems fallacious. If there is a case for running a particular element of public transport at a loss, the appropriate way of raising additional taxation (or cutting public expenditure) to meet it is to ask which additional tax etc., will have the best effects on the allocation of resources, the distribu-tion of income, and so on. In some circumstances (e.g. if the aim is to slow down the rate of contraction of a railway system) it may make sense to subsidize railways and to levy temporary additional taxes on roads. But as a general principle there is no more reason why road users alone should subsidise rail users than fish eaters alone should subsidise meat eaters.

The next subject is whether it is more appropriate for the government to borrow rather than tax to meet the costs of any subsidisation. We argued in chapter 2[72] that one reason for a deficit might be the contribution of facilities benefiting a future generation and that, if so, financial arrangements which throw the burden on a future generation, rather than on the present one, would be appropriate.[73] There are two distinct sets of ways in which it can be argued that debt-raising would fulfil this role better than taxation.[74]

Ever since Ricardo, it has been argued that if the present generation cuts capital formation more in response to a given levy in debt form than to the same levy in tax form, a burden is thrown on future generations, in the sense that they inherit a smaller physical capital stock. The essence of this reasoning is that any one individual may feel richer with a government bond certificate plus a vague obligation to service the bond in the future than with a tax receipt; so he will cut his consumption less in the first case, thereby implying a larger cut in saving, than in the second case. The second argument, or set of arguments, is much more recent. One version is that in contrast to taxation, lending is an act of voluntary exchange and so cannot involve any current burden. Hence the burden of debt raised by one generation rests on future generations, in the particular sense that the hands of the latter are tied to the extent that to service or repay this debt they have to pay more taxes than they otherwise would have done. Another version is to put the emphasis on the overlapping of generations and to argue that in such cases public borrowing can be undertaken without any final reduction in net worth to the first generation – in that any initial reduction in consumption may be compensated by a burden transfer to the second generation during the period of overlap. Finally, it must be understood that both the long and the recently recognised mechanisms of burden transfer can be operating simultaneously; they are in no sense mutually exclusive.

However, all these shifting arguments seem to envisage an active bond market in which government stock is freely bought by individuals. When it is much more a question of financial intermediaries subscribing to bonds, and even then sometimes under duress, the relevance of some of these arguments is not so clear. Furthermore, the assumption common to all these discussions is that full employment of an economy, neither more nor less, is assured so that no public stabilisation policy is needed. Although it can be argued that the Keynesian unemployment mechanism does not operate in the same way in the developing countries of Africa as in, say, the United States it is clear that these countries are all very familiar today with other aspects of fluctuations in aggregate demand. One must therefore conclude that the applicability of these arguments about shifting burdens on to future generations is extremely limited in our present context.

Another question is whether central or local governments should provide the necessary financial assistance to a public enterprise. The main point here is straightforward: if the benefits from the subsidy are clearly identifiable as local in character, there is a case for meeting the deficit from local resources.[75] But sometimes benefits will be diffused through several or many local authority areas. And whether they are or not, the principle of meeting them from local finance may be an empty one if the system is that the local authority only raises a small amount of funds by local taxation and obtains the rest in the form of grants from the central government. There may also be other disadvantages of a tactical nature in developing countries. Insofar as international aid is more likely to be forthcoming to help out central rather than local imbalances, there will be a case for emphasising the former rather than the latter.

Much of our discussion of public transport subsidies has been based on an implicit assumption which we must now question. Public enterprises are usually financed entirely through fixed interest stocks and so there is no cushion to meet a fall in demand. But if it were possible to finance them by an equity element as well as a bond element, there would be a cushion. One particular suggestion here seems worth exploring. In evidence before the *Radcliffe Committee* in the United Kingdom in the 1950s, Professor E. Victor Morgan[76] suggested that the UK nationalised industries might issue stocks on which dividends would be linked to sales rather than profits, subject to a guaranteed minimum. Although holders of such stocks would not have voting rights, they would at least have some hedge against inflation. No doubt this particular suggestion must be tailored to fit the needs of individual countries. (E.g., would it be better to link dividends to volume or value of sales? If the latter, would governments be tempted to control prices of public enterprises so as to keep down dividends? And would there be a market of

143

any size for such stocks?) But it does at least seem worth rather more consideration than it has received so far.

Transport Accounting

When outlining the administrative framework lying behind our suggestions on transport charging, etc., we promised to return to the subject of transport accounting later. We shall now deal successively with the general form that accounting should take, the arguments for and against earmarking of transport revenues for transport expenditures and the pattern of grants for transport purposes to local authorities.

Form of accounts

Whether the executive organisation for transport is a section of a government department or a separate public agency, it is necessary to set up a form of accounts on commercial principles, distinguishing clearly between current and capital transactions. If the common form of accounts for other government departments is on a cash basis rather than on an accruals basis and without any distinction between current and capital transactions, it may be necessary for parliamentary purposes to have an alternative classification in such form. But there should be no question that the commercial form of accounting is the one for operational purposes. There is plenty of scope for variation between countries – for instance, separate sets of accounts for road, rail, air, water transport, etc., where necessary, differing assumptions about depreciation, etc. – but the general principle is clear.

The detailed form such accounts should take is more a matter for the accountant than the economist but the sort of thing we have in mind is the pattern suggested some years ago for the UK government trading departments by Sir John Hicks.[77] He suggested that there should be a trading account in which current incomings and outgoings plus depreciation were entered; a

144

profit and loss account with trading profits and subsidies (if any) on one side with interest payments on the other; and finally a capital account which shows depreciation provisions (from the trading account) and surplus of profit (from the profit and loss account) together with other incomings such as loans proceeds while putting gross investment, debt repayment, increases in cash balances, etc. together on the other side. No doubt, one can play many variations on this theme, but it does exemplify the general principles.

Earmarking

The next question is the precise composition of the items to be entered on the receipts and outlay side of the accounts, and the relation between them.

As the outlay side is simpler, let us deal with that first. One needs to enter all the obvious items of current expenditure (wages, salaries, materials, etc.) together with appropriate estimates of interest and depreciation (the latter being on a replacement cost basis, as argued earlier) along with capital expenditure. In addition, if one is to have a true and proper picture of total relevant outlay, one needs to enter any imputed expenditures in respect of costs relating to roads, public expenditure in coping with road accidents, the appropriate contribution to general revenue in respect of government 'overhead' expenditure, etc.

On the receipts side, there are three possibilities: general appropriations from Ministry of Finance funds, allocations of transport revenues or allocations of specific but non-transport revenues. Although there are many historical examples of the last possibility,[78] the main justification for such arrangements is when there is need for some enduring statutory division of funds, such as that between a central government and state or local governments. Where political cohesion can only be satisfied by a formal attribution of specific revenues to the constituent parts of a governmental structure, this device may be necessary. But, otherwise, the price to be paid in terms of inflexibility does not seem worthwhile.[79]

If we rule out assignment of non-transport revenues, the choice then lies between general appropriations and assignment of transport revenues. Given the general theme throughout this chapter and the preceding ones that one should apply public enterprise principles to transport pricing, it would seem much more appropriate to steer all the sorts of direct and indirect charges we have discussed directly into the transport accounts. It is then much more likely that the actions of those guiding these public transport operations will be geared to the sorts of policy principles we have set forth than if their revenues came to them second-hand, as it were. So this means that in the case of roads one would include not only the obvious items like gasoline taxes, vehicle licences, etc., but also customs and excise duties on vehicles, special charges (if any) for access to property or increments in land values, charges for services to other government departments (e.g., military vehicles should, when possible, be charged with road taxes, just like private vehicles) and so on.

We now come to the precise relationship between the receipts and outlay sides. This needs rather full discussion as it brings us to the heart of the arguments about earmarking of receipts towards specific expenditures. There are different senses in which the concept of earmarking can be interpreted, but we shall use it here to mean not only a state of affairs where specific revenues are allocated to the finance of specific expenditures, but where there is a relationship of equality between the two. In other words, we now want to ask whether it is appropriate that transport expenditures should be exactly related to transport revenues. Such a question is capable of various interpretations: whether the rule should apply to each section or branch of public transport, whether it should apply in each and every year, or over a period of years, and so on. We shall try to keep these various meanings in mind as we proceed.

There are two very different sorts of arguments by which earmarking of transport revenues for transport expenditures may be defended. The first is exemplified by Buchanan[80] who argues

146

that earmarking may, under certain conditions, be a better means of registering and implementing individual preferences than general fund budgeting. Earmarking may be thought of as a means of compartmentalising fiscal decisions. And whereas by this means the individual can (as in a freely operating market economy) adjust the relative quantities of the various publicly provided goods as he wishes, general fund budgeting is more analogous to a tie-in sale where the individual purchaser does not have this same freedom.

The second type of argument is exemplified by Lewis[81] who puts the case for earmarking on the grounds that taxpayers will be more amenable to parting with their money in this case, e.g., if they can see a new road being built and understand that the road charges they are paying are being specifically allocated for this purpose, taxpayer compliance will be that much greater. He is aware of the drawbacks to earmarking funds in this way, but argues that the gains outweigh the losses. This sort of argument is often extended by saying that it is particularly at the local level that one may reap these advantages.

Therefore, we have two kinds of arguments for earmarking transport revenues for transport expenditures: one is that it is a better means of registering individual preferences through the budgetary machinery and the other is that it is a means of expanding the size of the public sector – a somewhat ill-matched pair of bedfellows!

The third type of argument is essentially political: that it is a good thing to tie the hands of politicians by ensuring that a substantial proportion of revenue is devoted to 'good' ends so that the scope for 'wasting' it is reduced. One can sympathise with this view – the most casual acquaintance with some governments at some times is sufficient for that – but at the same time there are some very real snags about it. Who is to lay down the distinction between 'good' and 'bad' objects of spending, if one does not trust the political leaders of a government to do it? And even if the distinction is once made, how can one really ensure that it is not evaded or that it does not soon become obsolete? All in all, it would not seem that this view-point can really command a lot of support.

So much for the arguments for earmarking, and their strengths and weaknesses. The main argument against earmarking in the sense used here is implicit in our previous discussion. We have argued that there are some cases in which public transport should be run at a loss and some in which it should make a surplus, for either allocative or distributional reasons. We have also argued that, although transport authorities should price their products in such a way as to make some contribution towards capital expenditure from surpluses on revenue account, recourse to borrowing is perfectly legitimate when there is a particularly heavy capital programme to be met. So even though one should accept the principle of allocating transport revenues to a transport account rather than to the general funds of government, the further step of relating revenue to expenditure in a mechanical or precise fashion does not seem justifiable. In some circumstances, it will be appropriate to credit a surplus to general government funds; in some to receive a subsidy from them; and in others, to receive or repay loans.

Quite apart from this, there are some awkward problems of averaging. One might reasonably argue for a separation of road and rail. But at the other extreme, is one to account for Oxford Street separately from Regent Street in London? There is a real dilemma here. If one argues for a minute sub-division – and this argument would presumably apply to education, health and a lot of other things as well as transport – one then ends up with a large number of separate government funds and, in effect, no overall budget at all. And if one does not have this minute division, one then may have lending and borrowing between different segments of transport so that there is not necessarily any close relation between individual preferences and actual expenditures, even over an extended period of time.[82]

A further point is that those who argue for earmarking on the grounds of preserving individual preferences may neglect a boomerang effect. Historically, transport expenditure has sometimes been a means by which governments extended their influence over the territories under their control. There are both recent[83] and older[84] examples of this.

In view of all this, one must feel some reluctance in giving wholehearted support to earmarking despite the arguments often put forward in its favour.[85]

Particular point can be given to these general conclusions by the example of Kenya. The system of operating a Road Fund fed, in part at any rate, from earmarked funds was tried from 1950 to 1963, but was then abandoned on the grounds that it imposed too great an element of inflexibility on government financial operations. Appendix 4B shows some of the details.[86]

Local authority grants
Grants from the central government to local authorities can either be of a general character related to yardsticks such as size of population, level of income, percentage of unemployment, etc. or alternatively they may be earmarked for specific expenditure such as roads, education, and so on. There are many historical examples of grants being given or proposed for transport purposes.[87]

The merits and demerits of earmarking (and the different forms of earmarking) grants from central to local governments have been discussed for many years[88] and it would be excessively tedious to recapitulate them in detail. The main points are the relative competence of central and local bodies; the circumstances under which the central government may have a better view of needs in a particular area than the local authority (e.g., where roads have to be part of a national network); the advantages of stimulating local initiative, and so on. It is hard to avoid the extremely vague conclusion that there must be some cases in which earmarking is fully justified, but that one cannot say it should be allowed *carte blanche*.

149

Conclusions

We have concentrated largely on the means of fulfilling the twin objectives of better price/cost alignment and deficit minimisation. It can be argued that public enterprises should not just minimise deficits, but actually earn substantial surpluses to help finance general capital accumulation; but it can also be said that there are some countries (e.g., Brazil) which have been notoriously lax in transport charging but have nevertheless grown at a fast rate. So it did not seem to us that growth arguments give a clear lead on this point. Nor did we feel that income distribution objectives could be given a primary role on a par with those of resource allocation.

There is a whole series of direct and indirect methods of charging which may be used as appropriate. But it must be clearly understood that in the present state of knowledge and with the present lack of technical personnel, close alignment between prices and marginal costs is far from easy. In the near future, all one can hope for in many cases is a rather better association between prices and average costs for particular services, but as time goes on one would certainly want to move progressively closer to a system of marginal cost pricing. It is recognised that there are some cases, whether intentional or unintentional, where deficits may be justified. Although bottlenecks or excess demand would enable surpluses to be made, it seems unlikely that cases of this sort will outnumber the former. So this may well mean that some small overall degree of subsidisation from general funds is necessary.

In addition to these main topics we have discussed the sorts of ways in which subsidies should be applied and the implications of raising the necessary finance from public loans rather than taxes. We have also explored some of the issues of transport accounting. Finally, it should be remembered that all these arguments were developed against a background of specific assumptions about administrative arrangements of public enterprises, their relationships to central government departments, and so on.

What of the future? The first point which emerges from our study is how little is known about public transport. We are very much aware of the limitations – both in terms of scope and reliability – of the data in chapter 3 and its appendices. But a very large number of manhours was spent in making even this meagre catch. So one cannot stress too frequently or too loudly how much more we need to know about what happens at present before we can pronounce with any great confidence on the past or undertake detailed predictions about the future. And this in turn points to the general need for specifying more fully the sort of data needed and to the particular need for the training and employment of many more people capable of making costing studies and the like. Appendix 4C sets out the desirable statistical information in some detail.

Even though the fog is pretty dense, one or two shapes can be dimly perceived through it. One is the ways in which the experiences of developing countries may well differ from those of developed countries: the most obvious is the relative role of rail and road transport. As the developing countries of today have never been as fully provided with railways as the west – certainly in terms of track mileage per head of population and possibly relatively to the volume of potential traffic – some of the problems experienced by the latter should be avoidable. If there is willingness to learn and to experiment, it may also be possible to avoid some of the further complications arising from own-account transport (e.g., the operation of minibuses by municipalities might provide a better alternative to private cars than standard buses; the variants on standard taxi-cab arrangements which one finds in cities as different as Istanbul and Addis Ababa suggests that there is a real demand for such services). But the phrase 'willingness to learn and to experiment' must be emphasised. It is no good having lessons from the west or, for that matter, their own past mistakes, staring people in the face if they are too slothful or too traditionally minded to learn from such lessons or to translate their learning into action. And in view of some of the findings in chapter 3, one cannot be wholly

F

151

optimistic on this score or be very sure about the likelihood of the acceptance of the relatively modest proposals we have put forward.

It seems likely that developing countries are going to experience (and, in fact, are already doing so) the pull to the towns which has characterised many western countries. We have suggested various ways in which transport pricing could be devised to exercise some pull in the other direction. But, assuming that it will happen to some considerable extent, there are some obvious lessons to be learned, such as joint consideration of transport networks and town planning arrangements, the provision and operation of mass transit arrangements, the purchase of land for new highway construction well before it is commonly known to be needed (to economise on cost), the development of short-cut procedures for compulsory purchase (to economise on time and cost), and so on. All such arguments reinforce the need, already stressed in this monograph, for the overall responsibility for transport matters resting with one ministry alone rather than with a plurality. Without this, there is no hope of any rational system of transport pricing and finance.

But perhaps the most important lesson of all is the irreversibility of much government action in this field. Once the state has introduced subsidies or imposed restrictions on transport operations which benefit particular interests, they are extremely hard to put into reverse, let alone eliminate, whether the interests concerned are private (e.g., concessionary fares) or public (e.g., taking over private transport undertakings). It is easy to forget that such arrangements soon become the natural order of things to the administering bureaucrats as well as to the ostensible beneficiaries. So the corollary must be that the economist's basic plea always has to be for a good dose of competitive pricing principles; if he does not stand up and be counted on their behalf, no one else will.

Appendix 4A

Transport Regulation

Arguments for and against road licencing restrictions have recently been fully discussed in the Geddes Committee *Report* in the United Kingdom[89] and we do not propose to cover the whole field here. There are a number of economic arguments in favour of licencing in one form or another. The first is that it may be a means of helping the railways in the transitional period while they are adjusting their tariffs on to a cost basis [90] or while they are being freed from various outworn statutory obligations. And, insofar as it is necessary to retain some of these shackles indefinitely (e.g. an obligation to provide standby or emergency services) it could be argued that there is a case for permanent and not just temporary restriction of road vehicles. It seems reasonable to draw distinctions between temporary and permanent restrictions and between existing ones and new ones. If there already are restrictions, and if it will be some years before railways can adjust their tariffs, there may be a case for retaining the restrictions, or for only loosening them slowly. If, on the other hand, such restrictions are not already in being or if there are reasons why, even in the long run, one must expect the railways to operate at a loss in accounting terms, then surely the right policy is to face the deficit openly rather than attempt to reduce it, at the cost of introducing other inefficiencies into the economy.

The second argument for restrictions is that they may reduce tax avoidance and evasion: if vehicle operators have to apply for a licence for a truck to carry goods as well as for it to go on the road, this will ensure greater compliance with the law. This is clearly a matter of tax administration and so one must be hesitant in saying that it has no force anywhere. But it hardly seems a strong enough argument on its own to warrant the application of these procedures.

Another argument[91] is that if the supply of trucks available is limited by import controls etc., the abolition of licencing would simply mean an excess demand for them. The logic of this is not entirely clear. If there is a ready demand for the services provided by licenced trucks, one is saying that those fortunate enough to get licences can

153

make high profits; the abolition of the licencing procedure would mean that fortune smiles instead on those who can get trucks – not obviously a better, or worse, group than the first.

There are many other arguments for licencing (e.g., the proposition that there would be too many entries to the industry or too few exits from it, or both) but these are not germane to our particular interests here. There are also many arguments against licencing which, although extremely important (e.g., the powers of political patronage conferred thereby; and the impediments to indigenous enterprise) do not concern us directly, but there are one or two which must be singled out for discussion. One is the proposition, which we have encountered before, that it is appropriate for road users to subsidise rail users. It may be administratively convenient to organise assistance to the railways this way but the economic tests for deciding the source of a subsidy should be the usual ones of resource allocation, distribution, etc. It may simply happen that restrictions on road transport which reduce its supply, thereby increasing freight charges and presumably benefiting the railways, are a less harmful method of assistance than any other – but this would be a fortuitous result if it were so. And, in any case, this chain of events is by no means a reliable one in that the major result of such restrictions might be to help own-account operators rather than the railways.

Another point is that the government machinery in general, and hence the tax machinery in particular, is not helped by laws which are too expensive to administer in great detail and so are persistently flouted. We have seen that this is very much the case in Uganda with respect to passenger transport regulations; and the same seems to hold in respect of freight transport in Kenya. Disrespect for the law at one point can very easily lead to disrespect at other and more important points.

So by and large, the conclusion must be that on the basis of these arguments restrictive licencing does not have a great deal to commend it. Even if there were no other arguments to consider, this does not mean that it should necessarily be abolished immediately everywhere but simply that the emphasis should be on relaxation where it already exists and extreme caution about allowing such a Trojan Horse into new territory. The precise form that restrictive licencing should take, if it is judged necessary, is beyond our scope but it may be noted that there is at least one country in the world (The Lebanon) where licences are auctioned to the highest bidder. Raising more public revenue by taxing surpluses in this way is an excellent system which deserves to be copied in other countries, which for one reason or another impose restrictions on private operators.

Appendix 4B

Kenya Road Fund

In 1950 a Road Authority and Road Fund were set up with the following principal function[92]:

> to formulate, and be responsible for the execution of, the policy in relation to the planning classification, siting, construction, reconstruction, discontinuance, diversion, improvement, maintenance, and repair of all public roads.

It was provided that the Fund should be fed from statutory revenues (most licence and driving fees plus gasoline and diesel fuel revenues from the consumption tax)[93] together with additional discretionary revenues as needed. Expenditure might be for recurrent or non-recurrent purposes and might either be central government direct expenditures or central government grants to local authorities.

The detailed operations of the Road Fund can best be illustrated by taking the data for a single year and subsequently relating this to trends (see table 4B1, p. 157).

It can be seen from the table that the statutory contribution was not much more than half the total receipts in 1961–2. There is in fact little evidence to show that road expenditure in Kenya has been closely related to statutory revenue: the nearest approach to this seems to have been the idea that statutory revenue should be more or less sufficient to support current expenditures, but that, if it were a matter of less rather than more, there should be a special contribution to enable the Fund to balance on its current account operations. In fact, the special contribution was unusually small in 1961–2, being normally of the order of £200,000 a year in the 1950s. It was always envisaged that non-recurrent expenditure should be met by Development Fund or similar allocations.

To put the 1961–2 figures in perspective, it might be added that statutory revenue was £918,000 in 1954–5 and total revenue of all kinds £1,838,000. By and large, total expenditure was about the same as total revenue in most years but with small surpluses and deficits from one year to another.

The Road Fund was never responsible for *all* road expenditure in

156

Table 4·B1   Kenya Road Fund, 1961–2 (£,000)

Revenue	Amount	Expenditure		Amount
Statutory contributions	1,821	Adminstration		651
Special revenue contribution	9	Maintenance:		1,175
Development fund allocation	653	Direct	530	
Other development finance	740	Grants to local		
		authorities	645	
		Non-recurrent:		1,097
		Direct	700	
		Grants	397	
		Surplus		300
Total	3,223	Total		3,223

Source: Road Authority, *Annual Reports*.

Note: Other development finance includes extraordinary contributions such as £350,000 from the International Bank and £120,000 from the U K government.

Kenya as local authorities financed some from their own resources – at a rate of about £700,000 a year in the late 1950s and early 1960s. Nor has it ever had responsibility for such items as policing the roads; and although it was responsible for administration of contractor finance schemes, they are not reflected in its accounts.

In 1963, the statutory contribution to the Road Fund was abolished on the basis of recommendations by the IBRD Report,[94] and the *Economy* Commission of 1962. After that date, the Road Fund continued to discharge the same expenditure functions but its statutory contribution was replaced by a contribution from general revenue, allocated annually in accordance with the overall budgetary situation. It has therefore lost the particular fiscal significance which it enjoyed during the period from 1950 to 1963. But even for that period one must remember that statutory revenue was only part of the total and that there were various types of expenditure outside the ambit of the Fund.

Appendix 4C

General Note on Desirable Statistical Information on Transport

It is taken for granted that it will be useful to obtain data on the quantities of passengers and freight carried, on track and road mileages, and also on the number and distribution by class of vehicles used. Much of this data is available, at a fairly aggregated level, for rail transport – though not always readily accessible outside the countries concerned. The main deficiences in this type of information relate to road transport. Definitions of roads and tracks are not standardised, so that road mileage data has to be treated with caution. The same applies to the road vehicle estimates where the data supplied by the licencing authorities may not be reliable. Estimates of tonnages and ton-mileage classified by commodity and geographical area are generally non-existent or seriously deficient. The same holds for commodity classification of rail traffics and of geographical rail flows.

However, such traffic and operating data is of supplementary rather than primary use in this study. Of more direct relevance is financial data relating to railways and roads.

Aggregated accounting data for *railway operations* is normally available in the published reports of the relevant authorities, though in a number of instances the information was too compressed to be a great use for the present purpose. Ideally, the following types of financial information are required:

1. Gross receipts attributable to rail operations (in some instances these are not distinguished in the available published accounts from receipts attributable to ancillary transport activities).
2. Gross costs attributable to rail operations – distinguishing particularly depreciation charges, interest and debt redemption charges and general administrative charges. Discrepancies between actual depreciation charges and charges calculated on a replacement cost basis should be obtainable. So should subsidy or tax elements affecting costs.
3. Flow of funds analysis – indicating sources and uses of finance

over a period of time, and specifying borrowing terms, especially if funds obtained externally.

The three categories of data described so far should for the most part be obtained without too much difficulty but this data alone is too aggregated for pricing policy purposes.

4. More detailed rail cost information is required. It is difficult to generalise as to the best method or degree of disaggregation required though the most fruitful is likely to be according to route, commodity, journey length and/or consignment size. The information obtained in this way would be average cost data, based upon the avoidability principle, with respect to a specified time period. In many cases this cost figure will diverge from the 'direct' cost figure calculated by conventional rail costing techniques. Where the average cost estimate diverges substantially from the marginal cost estimate then the latter type of estimate should also be available.

It can be safely stated that in most rail systems of the world, not simply those in developing countries, such costing sophistication as implied above does not exist; nor do the systems possess the quantity of skilled personnel required to conduct this type of costing investigation. Nevertheless, there is some evidence – for example, East African Railways and Harbours – of a slow movement towards an awareness of the importance of more detailed costing; this could usefully be stimulated.

5. Disaggregated rail revenue data on the same basis as the cost data is required. In principle, this task is considerably easier. Frequently the data is not available in the most suitable form because the appropriate accounting procedures for the collection and processing of sales information have not been established.

Financial data relating to *roads*, even at the aggregate level, is not readily accessible. The following items appear to be the most urgently necessary:

1. Total annual revenues derived from road users – classified according to level of government authority (data problems being much greater below central government level) and according to type of payment (licence duties, vehicles and parts, import duties, fuel duties).

F*

2. Total annual costs incurred in road provision – classified according to type of cost (maintenance, policing, administration, capital expenditure).

3. Flow of funds analysis – indicating sources and uses of finance over a period of time, and specifying borrowing terms, especially if funds are obtained externally.

4. As in the case of rail operations, more disaggregated cost and revenue data is required and for the same reasons. Information should be obtained on the variations in road user charges per vehicle-mile for different types of vehicles operating on different types of roads. Equally necessary, but much harder to obtain, is average road costs per vehicle-mile on different types of route (with different gradients, subsoil and surface) and with different traffic densities. Much work has been done in this field in the USA (e.g. AASHO studies); and more recently pioneer work has come from the Road Research Laboratory in developing countries and from the Ministry of Transport in the UK (e.g. *Road Track Costs*). There may be a strong case for establishing within transport ministries a division to collect this type of information.

Notes

1 Cf. Carlin, *op. cit.*, p. 434,
2 Cf. below, p. 145.
3 Cf. below, p. 130.
4 Cf. above, pp. 65 and 71.
5 See above, p. 35.
6 From the viewpoint of calculating the costs of operations performed in a particular way. We do not explore at this point the arguments about whether the particular ways found in practice are too capital-intensive, because of over-estimation of labour costs or under-estimation of capital costs.
7 Louis Lefeber and M.Datta Chauduri, *loc. cit.*
8 Ministry of Transport and Communications, *Report of Road Transport Reorganisation Committee*, Delhi, 1959.
9 Surveys and Research Corporation, *Indian Coal Transport Study*, appendix C, supplementary paper 3, 'The Cost of Capital in India'.
10 Whether further modifications should be made to actual costs to allow for balance of payments disequilibrium at current rates of exchange depends on such issues as whether governments are aiming at dispensing with foreign aid in the foreseeable future and whether all public agencies are operating on the basis of a common shadow exchange rate.
11 This is a necessary but not a sufficient condition for optimum pricing policy for public transport. If one divides the economy into three sectors (say, public transport, private transport and the rest) and if the price/marginal cost ratio diverges from unity, to differing extents in the latter two cases, then whatever ratio is chosen for the first sector must be out of line with one of the latter two. Cf. above, p. 47.

This point is analogous to the standard proposition in tax theory that if one has three commodities, x, y, and z (z being leisure), then neither a general income tax nor a specific excise tax on either x or y will leave the marginal equivalences unchanged, e.g., an excise tax on x will upset that between x and (y, z) and a general income tax, that between (x, y) and z.

12 This was the conclusion reached in Ministry of Transport, *Report of Committee on Carriers' Licencing*, HMSO, London, 1965, chapter 12; the argument has since been taken further in *Road Track Costs*. We have not found any information of substance on this subject in any of the countries investigated.

13 It can be argued that in principle short-run marginal costs are preferable when capacity is markedly under-utilised or overstrained. But the main example of the latter in the case of roads is when congestion costs arise; for reasons we shall come to shortly, we see no prospect of charging on this basis in developing countries in the foreseeable future. Therefore application of SRMC pricing would be confined to the under-utilisation case and so would lead to substantial deficits – to an extent likely to be in conflict with the need to minimise calls on general government funds.

14 Transportation Consultants Inc., *Transportation Survey of Sierra Leone*, Washington, DC, March 1963, p. 35.

15 There are many examples of such practices; A.M.Martin and W.A.Lewis, 'Patterns of Public Revenue and Expenditure', *The Manchester School*, September 1956, made the point that the application of western-level personal income tax rates in developing countries will not produce the same tax/income ratio as in western countries, simply because the mean level of income is much lower. To get the same tax/income ratio, one would need to apply western tax rates to the same *relative* (rather than to the same *absolute*) positions in the income scale – a man with an income of $1,000 per annum is well off by Indian standards whereas, on this income, tax liabilities in the United States would be very small.

Similarly, if one aims at incorporating a progressive element into customs and excise taxes on private road vehicles, the same principle will hold. It is no good reserving such taxes for large cars and exempting everything else (small cars, motor cycles, bicycles, bullock carts, rickshaws, and the like) if the aim is to have a high ratio of tax to consumption expenditure.

16 Carlin, *op. cit.*, p. 439.

17 In 1953, for instance, it was estimated that a half-ton vehicle paid a tax equivalent to 230 per cent of the infrastructure costs it imposed whereas a 15-tonner only paid 66 per cent (Brian T.

Bayliss, *European Transport*, Mason, London, 1965, p. 43). But proposals for substantial increases in charges on heavy vehicles have recently been made in the UK, France and West Germany (cf. Ministry of Transport, *The Transport of Freight*, Cmnd. 3470, HMSO, London, November 1967).

18 Cf. *Road Track Costs*, especially chapter 8 and relevant annexes. The potentialities of a tax related to the number of axles per vehicle are also discussed there.

19 Cf. Arthur Hazlewood, *Rail and Road Costs in East Africa*, Blackwell, Oxford, 1964, p. 151.

20 French car licencing charges are based on a combination of age and horsepower. Charges for a five-year old vehicle are half what they would be for a new one.

21 Cf. appendix 4A for an example.

22 *Op. cit.*, p. 327. But see E.K.Hawkins, *op. cit.*, p. 91, for some contrary opinions.

23 See, e.g., J.F.Due, *Sales Taxation*, Routledge and Kegan Paul, London, 1957, for full discussion.

24 The argument in *Road Track Costs*, chapter 4 and annex 16, that one should not include purchase taxes, etc. in road charging systems, on the grounds that the amount paid is unrelated to use, is tantamount to a dismissal of two-part pricing techniques. And the distinction drawn between licence charges (acceptable) and purchase tax (not acceptable) seems extremely thin.

25 Above, p. 59.

26 Cf. *Report of Motor Vehicle Taxation Enquiry Committee*, New Delhi, 1950, and *Report of Local Finance Enquiry Committee*, New Delhi, 1951.

27 *Local Finance Enquiry Committee.*

28 Cf. above, p. 116.

29 Chapter 2, pp. 31, and appendix 2A.

30 Cf. J.M.Thomson, 'An Evaluation of Two Proposals for Traffic Restraint in Central London', *Journal of the Royal Statistical Society*, part 3, 1967.

31 *Committee on Transport Policy*, pp. 71–2.

32 See, e.g., J.R.Sargent, *Report on Transport Requirements in the Light of Economic Development in North Borneo*, Information Office, Jesselton, North Borneo, 1960.

33 Provided that political conditions are not such that dismissals of redundant labour would be impossible anyway.

34 The Sierra Leone *Transportation Survey* made this point (p. 48).

35 *Op. cit.*, p. 74.

36 Gerald K.Helleiner, *Peasant Agriculture, Government and Economic Growth in Nigeria*, Irwin, Homewood, Illinois, 1966, p. 261.

37 *Op. cit.*, p. 264.

38 Cf. Carlin, *op. cit.*, for detailed arguments in the case of India.

39 Cf. Hazlewood, *op. cit.*, p. 140. And for India see *Report of Committee on Transport Policy and Coordination*, p. 316.

40 The scope for such changes is illustrated by Bonavia (*ibid.*, p. 322), who makes the point that the average distance between stations in India (five miles) is related to bullock cart transport. An appropriate spacing for motor transport would be 20–30 miles.

41 It can be argued that this is a service which should enter into prices; but it is not easy to visualise this principle being translated into practice (cf. Burton A.Weisbrod, 'Collective-Consumption Services of Individual-Consumption Goods', *Quarterly Journal of Economics*, August 1964).

42 As shown in appendix 3C.

43 *Op. cit.*, p. 181.

44 United Nations Economic Commission for Africa, *Transport Problems in Relation to Economic Development in West Africa*, Addis Ababa, 1962, chapter 5. See also Jan de Weille, *Quantification of Road User Savings*, Occasional Papers No. 2, International Bank, Washington DC, 1966.

45 E.K.Hawkins, 'Investment in Roads in Underdeveloped Countries', *Oxford Bulletin of Statistics*, November 1960, p. 367.

46 Cf. Sir Arthur Lewis, 'A Review of Economic Development', *American Economic Review*, May 1965, pp. 12ff. for detailed discussion.

47 With some reservations about the precise end-result, cf. Hazlewood, *op. cit.*, chapter 9.

48 It would clearly be impracticable to make the differentials large.

49 *The Financial and Economic Obligations of the Nationalised Industries*, Cmnd. 1337, HMSO, London, April 1961. A subsequent

restatement is in *Nationalised Industries: A Review of Economic and Financial Objectives*, Cmnd. 3437, November 1967.

50 Cf. Tibor Scitovsky, 'Two Concepts of External Economies', *Journal of Political Economy*, April 1954, and Roland N. McKean, *Efficiency in Government Through Systems Analysis*, Wiley, New York, 1958, chapter 8, for a thorough discussion.

51 See Pan-American Union, *Farm to Market Roads in Latin America*, 1964, for further details.

52 Cf. Taxation Enquiry Committee (1953–4), Government of India, Delhi, 1955, vol. III, chapter 7; and also G.V.N. Reddy, 'A Note on Pricing in Irrigation Projects', *Indian Economic Review*, August 1957.

53 If one subscribes to the principle of assigned revenues, one can find a reason for tying any tax proceeds to transport expenditure. We shall deal with this point later. Cf. below, p. 145.

54 They are also a means of distributing public utility services (electricity, etc.) to property. Cf. *Road Track Costs*.

55 Net of any disadvantages, such as proximity to noise and fumes of traffic.

56 Cf. Ursula K. Hicks, *Development from Below*, Clarendon Press, Oxford, 1961, and also papers by Daniel M. Holland, Oliver Oldman, and Richard M. Bird in 1965 *Proceedings of National Tax Association*, Harrisburg, 1966.

57 Cf. Hawkins, *op. cit.*, p. 21, for the traditional system in Uganda, and above, p. 62, in respect of Ethiopia.

58 A.R. Prest and R. Turvey, *op. cit.*, p. 688.

59 Cf. G.K. Helleiner, *op. cit.*, chapter 4, for illustrations of the effects of the rail link to the coast in opening up the Kano area of Northern Nigeria in 1911–12; and the further effects of the recent railway extension to Bornu.

60 For further elaboration of many of these arguments see Highway Research Board, *Highway Research Record No. 20 – Highway Financing*, National Research Council, Washington DC, 1963.

61 See A.R. Prest, *Public Finance in Theory and Practice* (3rd ed.), Weidenfeld and Nicolson, London, 1967, chapter 14, for a short account.

62 Roughly, increments in land capital value due to permission to develop are to be taxed at 40 per cent (and probably 50 per cent

in a few years' time) while the maximum rate for long-term capital gains of other sorts is 30 per cent.

63 Cf. chapter 2, p. 17.

64 The precise relationship will depend on whether there are increasing, decreasing or constant returns in highway expansion. See Oswald H. Brownlee, 'Optimal Expenditure for Highways', International Institute of Public Finance, *Efficiency in Government Spending*, Saarbrücken, 1967.

65 This is a major justification of the Victoria Line in London; cf. C.D. Foster and M.E. Beesley, 'Estimating the Social Benefits of Constructing an Underground Railway in London', *Journal of Royal Statistical Society*, part I, 1963.

66 One example of such limitations is the difficulty experienced in recent years by East African Railways in raising loans to buy new rolling stock. Another is the gradual disappearance of the Contractor Finance schemes popular in African countries in recent years. Essentially, these were a means of short-term borrowing from contractors engaged in road works, the contractors in turn arranging external finance. Experience has shown, however, the difficulties of controlling the standards of construction work in cases where contractors were putting up the funds and so the system now seems to be on its way out.

67 E.g., as a European example, West Germany has preferred to make grants to enable people to move to West Berlin rather than subsidise travel costs (Bayliss, *op. cit.*, p. 123, note).

68 Cf. Lyle C. Fitch and Associates, *Urban Transportation and Public Policy*, Chandler, New York 1964, pp. 212ff.

69 N.S. Despicht, *op. cit.*, p. 76.

70 Cf. *White Paper*, Cmnd. 3057, *op. cit.*, and *Railway Policy*, Cmnd. 3439, *op. cit.* See also *Public Transport and Traffic*, Cmnd. 3481, HMSO, December 1967, for details of subsidies to public passenger road transport.

71 It might be noted that in considering the relative subsidies to be made to different sorts of public transport, the argument in favour of an equal absolute subsidy made by Fitch *et al* (*op. cit.*, pp. 161–7), seems to be based on the assumption of a larger amount of subsidy in one case than the other. This is surely invalid as a basis of comparison.

72 p. 21.

73 Presumably the accounting between the government and the public enterprise would in this case also take the form of a loan from one to the other.

74 Cf. C.S.Shoup, 'Debt Financing and Future Generations', *Economic Journal*, December 1962; Ferguson, *op. cit.*; Buchanan, *op. cit.*; R.A.Musgrave, *American Economic Review*, December 1965, p. 1228.

75 Cf. UK *White Paper*, Cmnd. 3057, p. 6, and also *White Paper*, Cmnd. 3481, p. 20.

76 *Committee on Working of the Monetary System*, Cmnd. 827, HMSO, London, August 1959, p. 220.

77 J.R.Hicks, *The Problem of Budgetary Reform*, Oxford University Press, Oxford, 1948. It should be added that he took the view that roads were a marginal case which could be accounted for on commercial principles or on traditional ones.

78 One is the 1888 system in the UK whereby some central revenues (certain licence receipts and a proportion of death duties) were allocated to local authority purposes. Among the revenues was that from licences issued to sellers of alcohol and among the expenditures was technical education. It is recorded that Sidney Webb, as chairman of the relevant committee of the London County Council, managed to persuade his colleagues that economics came under the heading 'technical' education and hence secured a grant which was a major contribution towards the founding of the London School of Economics (see Janet Beveridge, *An Epic of Clare Market*, Bell, London, 1960, chapter 2).

79 Cocoa subsidies in Trinidad are a good example. A system of allocating certain revenues to the cocoa industry started in the 1930s when the industry was very depressed. It continued to operate in a mechanical fashion throughout the 1940s and well into the 1950s despite the complete change in cocoa farmers' fortunes over the period. Cf. A.R.Prest, *A Fiscal Survey of the British Caribbean*, HMSO, London, 1957, p. 24.

80 James M.Buchanan, 'The Economics of Earmarked Taxes', *Journal of Political Economy*, December 1963.

81 Sir Arthur Lewis, *Development Planning*, Allen and Unwin, London, 1966, pp. 128–9.

82 An even worse situation is when one nominally has a lot of

separate funds but they are allowed to lend to one another, so that expenditure out of one is not really regulated by revenue flowing into it. Some experience with accounting in academic institutions suggests that this is by no means an impossible outcome.

83 New roads seem to have helped the Chinese in their suppression of the Tibetan rising (cf. B.Grossman, 'China's Transport Policy', in E.F.Szczepanik (ed.), *Economic and Social Problems of the Far East*, Hong Kong University Press, Hong Kong, 1962.

84 This was argued in respect of railway development in the nineteenth century in the United States, Canada and Russia (*Cambridge Economic History of Europe*, p. 250).

85 See, for instance, in addition to the general references above: Gabriel J.Roth, *A Self-Financing Road System*, Institute of Economic Affairs, London, 1966; C.Verburgh, *South African Transportation Policy*, Bureau of Economic Research, University of Stellenbosch, South Africa; and M.R.Bonavia, *Memorandum* in *Committee on Transport Policy*, p. 327. All these are specifically in respect of road transport.

86 It might also be noted that the idea of a Road Fund has been raised in Nigeria but decisively rejected, albeit on constitutional and administrative, rather than economic grounds (cf. Federal Government *Sessional Paper No.* 1, 1965).

87 Uganda operated an earmarked system until 1962, but then abandoned it on the grounds that the distribution of funds was too rigid and mechanistic (see *Memorandum* on *Financial Relationships*, appendix G. Report of Uganda Constitutional Conference, Cmnd. 1523, HMSO, London, October 1961). See also *Report of Committee on Transport Policy*, p. 67, for a proposal in respect of rural market roads in India.

88 In the UK, at least, ever since the *Report of the Royal Commission on Local Taxation*, 1899–1901, C9141 and C9142, HMSO, London, 1901.

89 Ministry of Transport, *Report of Committee on Carriers' Licencing, op. cit.* See also *The Transport of Freight*, Cmnd. 3470; and A.A.Walters, 'Economic Development and the Administration and Regulation of Transport', *Journal of Development Studies*, October 1967.

90 E.g., the argument often takes the form of saying that railway

costs over long distances are less than those by road for goods traffic but that tariffs frequently do not reflect this for historical reasons; cf. *Report of Madan Committee (Kenya)*.

91 Cf. Bonavia, *loc. cit.*, p. 321.

92 *Road Authority Ordinance*, 1950.

93 I.e., the additional tax needed to bring the Kenya taxes up to the common tariff level.

94 *Op. cit.*, p. 186, 'Because of the budgetary situation, arrangements for meeting maintenance costs should be decided annually by the government rather than by allocating receipts from specific taxes to the Road Fund'.

Subject Index

171